TRANSLATED

Translated Language Learning

The Fisherman and his Soul

漁師とその魂

Oscar Wilde

English / 日本語

Copyright © 2023 Tranzlaty
All rights reserved.
Published by Tranzlaty
ISBN: 978-1-83566-049-2
Original text by Oscar Wilde
The Fisherman and his Soul
First published in English in 1891
www.tranzlaty.com

The Mermaid
人魚

Every evening the young Fisherman went out to sea
毎晩、若い漁師は海に出かけました
and the young Fisherman threw his nets into the water
若い漁師は網を水に投げ入れました
When the wind blew from the land he caught nothing
大地から風が吹いてきたとき、彼は何も捕まえなかった
or he caught just a few fish at best
あるいは、せいぜい数匹の魚を捕まえただけだった
because it was a bitter and black-winged wind
それは苦い黒い翼の風だったからです
rough waves rose up to meet the wind from the land
荒波が立ち上り、陸からの風に応えた
But at other times the wind blew to the shore
しかし、風が岸に吹くこともありました
and then the fishes came in from the deep
すると、魚が深海からやって来ました
the fishes swam into the meshes of his nets
魚は彼の網の網の中を泳いでいった
and he took the fish to the market-place
そして、その魚を市場に持って行きました
and he sold all the fishes that he had caught
そして、捕まえた魚を全部売り払った

but there was one special evening
しかし、ある特別な夜がありました
the Fisherman's net was heavier than normal
漁師の網は普通より重かった
he could hardly pull his net onto the boat
彼は網をボートに引っ張るのがやっとでした
The Fisherman laughed to himself
漁師は独り笑いを浮かべた
"Surely, I have caught all the fish that swim"
「きっと、泳ぐ魚は全部捕まえた」
"or I have snared some horrible monster"

「恐ろしい怪物を罠にかけたか」
"a monster that will be a marvel to men"
「人間にとって驚異となる怪物」
"or it will be a thing of horror"
「さもないと恐ろしいことになる」
"a beast that the great Queen will desire"
「偉大なる女王が欲しがる獣」
With all his strength he tugged at the coarse ropes
彼は渾身の力を込めて粗いロープを引っ張った
he pulled until the long veins rose up on his arms
彼は腕の長い血管が浮き上がるまで引っ張った
like lines of blue enamel round a vase of bronze
青銅の花瓶を囲む青いエナメルの線のように
He tugged at the thin ropes of his nets
彼は網の細い縄を引っ張った
and at last the net rose to the top of the water
そしてとうとう網は水面に上がった
But there were no fish in his net
しかし、彼の網には魚がいなかった
nor was there a monster or thing of horror
また、怪物や恐ろしいものもいませんでした
there was only a little Mermaid
そこには小さな人魚しかいなかった
she was lying fast asleep in his net
彼女は彼の網の中でぐっすり眠っていた
Her hair was like a wet foil of gold
彼女の髪は濡れた金箔のようだった
like golden flakes in a glass of water
コップ一杯の水の中の金色のフレークのように
Her little body was as white ivory
彼女の小さな体は白い象牙のようだった
and her tail was made of silver and pearl
尻尾は銀と真珠でできていた
and the green weeds of the sea coiled round her tail
そして、海の緑の雑草が彼女の尻尾に巻き付いた
and like sea-shells were her ears
貝殻のように耳が彼女の耳だった

and her lips were like sea-coral
彼女の唇は海珊瑚のようだった
The cold waves dashed over her cold breasts
冷たい波が冷たい胸に押し寄せた
and the salt glistened upon her eyelids
そして塩が彼女のまぶたに光った
She was so beautiful that the he was filled with wonder
彼女はとても美しかったので、彼は不思議でいっぱいになりました
he pulled the net closer to the boat
彼は網をボートに近づけた
leaning over the side, he clasped her in his arms
横に身を乗り出し、彼は彼女を腕に抱きしめた
She woke, and looked at him in terror
彼女は目を覚まし、恐怖で彼を見た
When he touched her she gave a cry
彼が彼女に触れると、彼女は泣き叫びました
she cried out like a startled sea-gull
彼女は驚いたカモメのように叫んだ
she looked at him with her mauve-amethyst eyes
彼女は藤色のアメジストの瞳で彼を見た
and she struggled so that she might escape
そして、逃げようともがいた
But he held her tightly to him
しかし、彼は彼女をしっかりと抱きしめました
and he did not allow her to depart
そして、彼は彼女が去ることを許さなかった
She wept when she saw she couldn't escape
逃げられないのを見て泣いた
"I pray thee, let me go"
「お願いです、行かせてください」
"I am the only daughter of a King"
「私は王様の一人娘です」
"please, my father is aged and alone"
「お願い、お父さんは年老いて一人ぼっちなの」
But the young Fisherman would not let her go
しかし、若い漁師は彼女を手放そうとしませんでした

"I will not let thee go unless you make me a promise"
「約束しない限り、お前を逃がさない」
"whenever I call thee thou wilt come and sing to me"
「わたしがあなたを呼ぶときはいつでも、あなたは来てわたしのところに来て歌うであろう」
"because your song delights the fishes"
「あなたの歌が魚を喜ばせるから」
"they come to listen to the song of the Sea-folk"
「海の民の歌を聴きに来る」
"and then my nets shall be full"
「そうすれば、わたしの網はいっぱいになる」
the little mermaid saw that she had no choice
人魚姫は選択の余地がないことを悟りました
"Would thou truly let me go if I promise this?"
「これを約束したら、本当に私を行かせてくれるのですか?」
"In very truth I will let thee go," he premised
「まことに、わたしはおまえを行かせてやる」と彼は前提にした
So she made him the promise he desired
それで、彼女は彼が望む約束を彼にしました
and she swore to do it by the oath of the Sea-folk
そして彼女は海の民の誓いによってそれを誓った
the young Fisherman loosened his arms from the mermaid
若い漁師は人魚から腕を緩めました
the little mermaid sank back down into the water
人魚姫は水に沈みました
and she trembled with a strange kind of fear
そして、彼女は奇妙な恐怖に震えた

Every evening the young Fisherman went out upon the sea
毎晩、若い漁師は海に出て行きました
and every evening he called out to the mermaid
そして毎晩、人魚に声をかけました
the mermaid rose out of the water and sang to him
人魚は水から上がり、彼に歌いました
Round and round her swam the dolphins
ぐるぐる回ってイルカを泳がせた

and the wild gulls flew above her head
そして野生のカモメが彼女の頭上を飛んだ
she sang a marvellous song of the Sea-folk
彼女は海の民の素晴らしい歌を歌った
mermen who drive their flocks from cave to cave
洞窟から洞窟へと群れを駆逐する半魚人
mermen who carry the little calves on their shoulders
小さな子牛を肩に担ぐ半魚人
she sang of the Tritons who have long green beards
彼女は長い緑の髭を生やしたトリトンについて歌った
and she sang of the Triton's hairy chests
そして彼女はトリトンの毛むくじゃらの胸について歌った
they blow through twisted conchs when the King passes
王様が通るときにねじれた法螺貝を吹き飛ばします
she sang of the palace of the King
彼女は王の宮殿について歌った
the palace which is made entirely of amber
全体が琥珀でできている宮殿
the palace has a roof of clear emerald
宮殿には透明なエメラルドの屋根があります
and it has a pavement of bright pearl
そして、それは明るい真珠の舗装を持っています
and she sang of the gardens of the sea
そして彼女は海の園について歌った
gardens where great fans of coral wave all day long
一日中珊瑚の大ファンが波打つ庭園
and fish dart about like silver birds
そして、魚は銀色の鳥のように飛び回る
and the anemones cling to the rocks
そしてイソギンチャクは岩にしがみついています
She sang of the big whales that come from the north
彼女は北からやってくる大きなクジラのことを歌った
they have sharp icicles hanging from their fins
ヒレから鋭いつららがぶら下がっています
she sang of the Sirens who tell of wonderful things
彼女は素晴らしいことを語るセイレーンの歌を歌った
so wonderful that merchants block their ears with wax

あまりの素晴らしさに、商人たちは耳を蝋でふさぐほどです
they block their ears so that they can not hear them
耳をふさいで聞こえないようにするのです
because if they heard them they would leap into the water
なぜなら、もし彼らがそれを聞いたら、彼らは水に飛び込むだろうからです
and they would be drowned in the sea
そして、彼らは海で溺れ死ぬだろう
she sang of the sunken galleys with their tall masts
彼女は高いマストで沈没したガレー船のことを歌った
she sang of the frozen sailors clinging to the rigging
彼女は艤装にしがみつく凍りついた水兵たちの歌を歌った
she sang the mackerel swimming through shipwrecks
彼女は難破船の中を泳ぐ鯖を歌った
she sang of the little barnacles travelling the world
彼女は世界を旅する小さなフジツボを歌った
the barnacles cling to the keels of the ships
フジツボは船のキールにしがみついています
and the ships go round and round the world
そして船は世界をぐるぐる回る
and she sang of the cuttlefish in the sides of the cliffs
そして、崖の脇にいるイカのことを歌った
and they stretch out their long black arms
そして、長い黒い腕を伸ばします
they can make night come when they will it
歌詞の意味:
彼らは夜が来るときにそれを行うことができます。
She sang of the nautilus, who has a boat of her own
彼女は自分のボートを持っているノーチラス号のことを歌った
a boat that is carved out of an opal
オパールから彫り出されたボート
and the boat is steered with a silken sail
そして、ボートは絹の帆で操舵されます
she sang of the happy Mermen who play upon harps
彼女はハープを奏でる幸せな半魚人の歌を歌った
they can charm the great Kraken to sleep

彼らは偉大なクラーケンを眠らせることができます
she sang of the little children riding the porpoises
彼女はネズミイルカに乗った小さな子供たちのことを歌った
the little children laugh as the ride the porpoises
小さな子供たちはネズミイルカに乗って笑う
she sang of the Mermaids who lie in the white foam
彼女は白い泡の中に横たわる人魚について歌った
and they hold out their arms to the mariners
そして、彼らは船員たちに腕を差し出します
she sang of the sea-lions with their curved tusks
彼女は湾曲した牙を持つアシカの歌を歌った
and she sang of the sea-horses with their floating manes
そして、たてがみを浮かべたタツノオトシゴの歌を歌った
When she sang the fishes came from the sea
彼女が歌うと、魚は海からやって来ました
the fish came to listen to her
魚は彼女の言うことを聞きに来ました
the young Fisherman threw his nets round them
若い漁師は網を投げました
and he caught as many fish as he needed
そして、必要なだけ魚を捕まえました

when his boat was full the Mermaid sunk back down
彼のボートがいっぱいになると、マーメイド号は再び沈んでしまいました
she went back down into the sea smiling at him
彼女は彼に微笑みながら海へと戻っていった
She never got close enough for him to touch her
彼女は彼が彼女に触れるほど近づくことはありませんでした
Often times he called to the little mermaid
しばしば彼は人魚姫に呼びかけました
and he begged to her to come closer to him
そして、自分に近づくように彼女に懇願しました
but she dared not come closer to him
しかし、彼女は敢えて彼に近づかなかった
when he tried to catch her she dived into the water
彼が彼女を捕まえようとしたとき、彼女は水に飛び込みまし

た
just like when a seal dives into the sea
アザラシが海に飛び込むときのように
and he wouldn't see her again that day
そして、その日、彼は二度と彼女に会うことはなかった

each day her voice became sweeter to his ears
日を追うごとに、彼女の声は彼の耳に甘くなっていった
Her voice so sweet that he forgot his nets
彼女の声はとても甘く、彼は網を忘れた
and he forgot his cunning and his craft
そして、彼は自分の狡猾さと技術を忘れてしまった
The tuna went past him in large shoals
マグロは大きな群れで彼の横を通り過ぎた
but he didn't pay any attention to them
しかし、彼はそれらに注意を払わなかった
His spear lay by his side, unused
彼の槍は未使用のまま、彼の傍らに横たわっていた
and his baskets of plaited osier were empty
そして、編み物のオシエの籠は空っぽだった
With lips parted, he sat idle in his boat
唇を離して、彼はボートの中でぼんやりと座っていた
he listened to the songs of the mermaid
彼は人魚の歌に耳を傾けた
and his eyes were dim with wonder
そして、彼の目は驚きでぼんやりとしていました
he listened till the sea-mists crept round him
海霧が忍び寄るまで耳を澄ませた
the wandering moon stained his brown limbs with silver
彷徨う月が彼の茶色の手足を銀色に染めた

One evening he called to the mermaid
ある晩、彼は人魚に声をかけました
"Little Mermaid, I love thee," he professed
「リトル・マーメイド、愛してるよ」と彼は公言した
"Take me for thy bridegroom, for I love thee"
「わたしをあなたの花婿に連れて行ってください。わたしは

- 8 -

あなたを愛しています」
But the mermaid shook her head
だが人魚は首を横に振った
"Thou hast a human Soul," she answered
「あなたには人間の魂があるのよ」と彼女は答えた
"If only thou would send away thy Soul"
「汝の魂を送り出してくれさえすれば」
"if thy sent thy Soul away I could love thee"
「もしあなたがあなたの魂を送り出したなら、私はあなたを愛することができます」
And the young Fisherman said to himself
そして、若い漁師は自分に言いました
"of what use is my Soul to me?"
「わたしの魂は、わたしにとって何の役に立ちますか?」
"I cannot see my Soul"
「自分の魂が見えない」
"I cannot touch my Soul"
「私は自分の魂に触れることができない」
"I do not know my Soul"
「私は自分の魂を知らない」
"I will send my Soul away from me"
「私は私の魂を私から遠ざけます」
"and much gladness shall be mine"
「多くの喜びがわたしのものとなる」
And a cry of joy broke from his lips
そして、彼の唇から喜びの叫びが漏れた
he held out his arms to the Mermaid
彼は人魚に腕を差し出した
"I will send my Soul away," he cried
「私の魂を送り出します」と彼は叫んだ
"you shall be my bride, and I will be thy bridegroom"
「あなたはわたしの花嫁となり、わたしはあなたの花婿となる」
"in the depth of the sea we will dwell together"
「深海で共に暮らそう」
"all that thou hast sung of thou shalt show me"
「汝が歌ったものは、すべて我に見せよ」

"and all that thou desirest I will do for you"
「あなたが望むことはすべて、わたしがあなたのためにしてあげよう」
"our lives will not be divided no longer"
「私たちの人生はもう分断されません」
the little Mermaid laughed, full of delight
人魚姫は喜びに満ちて笑いました
and she hid her face in her hands
そして両手で顔を隠した
but the Fisherman didn't know how to send his Soul away
しかし、漁師は自分の魂を追い払う方法を知りませんでした
"how shall I send my Soul from me?"
「どうやって私の魂を私から送ればいいの?」
"Tell me how I can do it"
「どうすればできるのか教えて」
"tell me how and it shall be done"
「どのようにすれば、それが成し遂げられるのか教えてください」
"Alas! I know not" said the little Mermaid
「ああ!わたしは知らない」と人魚姫は言いました
"the Sea-folk have no Souls"
「海の民には魂がない」
And she sank down into the sea
そして彼女は海に沈んでいった
and she looked up at him wistfully
そして彼女は物憂げに彼を見上げた

The Priest
司祭

Early on the next morning
翌朝早く
before the sun was above the hills
太陽が丘の上に出る前に
the young Fisherman went to the house of the Priest
若い漁師は祭司の家に行きました
he knocked three times at the Priest's door
彼は司祭の戸を三度ノックした
The Priest looked out through the door
司祭は扉から外を覗いた
when he saw who it was he drew back the latch
それが誰であるかを見ると、彼は掛け金を引いた
and he welcomed the young Fisherman into his house
そして、若い漁師を家に迎え入れました
he knelt down on the sweet-smelling rushes of the floor
彼は甘い匂いのする床に膝をついた
and he cried to the Priest, "Father"
そして祭司に「父よ」と叫んだ
"I am in love with one of the Sea-folk"
「私は海の民の一人に恋をしている」
"and my Soul hindereth me from having my desire"
「わたしの魂は、わたしの望みを叶えるのを妨げている」
"Tell me, how I can send my Soul away from me?"
「教えてください、どうすれば私の魂を私から遠ざけることができますか?」
"I truly have no need of it"
「本当に必要ない」
"of what use is my Soul to me?"
「わたしの魂は、わたしにとって何の役に立ちますか?」
"I cannot see my Soul"
「自分の魂が見えない」
"I cannot touch my Soul"
「私は自分の魂に触れることができない」
"I do not know my Soul"

「私は自分の魂を知らない」
And the Priest beat his chest
そして僧侶は胸を叩いた
and he answered, "thou art mad"
すると彼は答えた、「あなたは気が狂っている」
"perhaps you have eaten poisonous herbs!"
「もしかしたら、毒草を食べたのかもしれない!」
"the Soul is the noblest part of man"
「魂は人間の最も高貴な部分である」
"and the Soul was given to us by God"
「そして、魂は神によって私たちに与えられました」
"so that we nobly use our Soul"
「魂を高貴に用いるために」
"There is no thing more precious than a human Soul"
「人間の魂ほど貴重なものはない」
"It is worth all the gold that is in the world"
「それは世界にあるすべての金の価値があります」
"it is more precious than the rubies of the kings"
「王のルビーよりも貴重だ」
"Think not any more of this matter, my son"
「息子よ、これ以上このことを考えるな」
"because it is a sin that may not be forgiven"
「赦されないかもしれない罪だから」
"And as for the Sea-folk, they are lost"
「そして、海の民は、道に迷った」
"and those who live with them are also lost"
「そして、彼らと一緒に暮らす人々もまた失われる」
"They are like the beasts of the field"
「彼らは野の獣のようだ」
"the beasts that don't know good from evil"
「善悪を知らない獣たち」
"the Lord has not died for their sake"
「主は彼らのために死なれたのではない」

he heard the bitter words of the Priest
彼は司祭の苦い言葉を聞いた
the young Fisherman's eyes filled with tears

若い漁師の目には涙があふれていました
he rose up from his knees and spoke, "Father"
彼は膝から立ち上がり、「父よ」と言った
"the fauns live in the forest, and they are glad"
「牧神は森に住んでいて、喜んでいる」
"on the rocks sit the Mermen with their harps of gold"
「岩の上には、金の竪琴を奏でる半魚人が座っている」
"Let me be as they are, I beseech thee"
彼らをそのままにさせてください、私はあなたに頼みます
"their days are like the days of flowers"
「彼らの日々は花の日々のようだ」
"And, as for my Soul," the young Fisherman continued
「そして、私の魂は」と若い漁師は続けた
 what doth my Soul profit me?"
わたしの魂は、わたしに何の益をもたらすのか。
"how is it good if it stands between what I love?"
自分の好きなものの間に立っているのに、どうしていいの？
"The love of the body is vile" cried the Priest
「肉体への愛は卑劣だ」と司祭は叫んだ
"and vile and evil are the pagan things"
「卑劣で邪悪なものは異教のものである」
"Accursed be the fauns of the woodland"
「森の牧神に呪われよ」
"and accursed be the singers of the sea!"
「海の歌い手は呪われよ!」
"I have heard them at night-time"
「夜に聞いたことがある」
"they have tried to lure me from my bible"
「彼らは私を聖書から引き離そうとしました」
"They tap at the window, and laugh"
「彼らは窓を叩いて笑う」
"They whisper into my ears at night"
「夜、耳元で囁かれる」
"they tell me tales of their perilous joys"
「彼らは危険な喜びの物語を私に語ってくれる」
"They try to tempt me with temptations"
「彼らは私を誘惑しようとする」

"and when I try to pray they mock me"
「そして、私が祈ろうとすると、彼らは私を嘲笑します」
"The mer-folk are lost, I tell thee"
「人魚の民は道に迷った、汝に告げよう」
"For them there is no heaven, nor hell"
「彼らには天国も地獄もない」
"and they shall never praise God's name"
「彼らは決して神の御名をほめたたえることはない」
"Father," cried the young Fisherman
「お父さん」と若い漁師は叫びました
"thou knowest not what thou sayest"
「汝は汝の言うことを知らない」
"Once in my net I snared the daughter of a King"
「一度、私は王様の娘を罠にかけた」
"She is fairer than the morning star"
「彼女は明けの明星よりも美しい」
"and she is whiter than the moon"
「そして、彼女は月よりも白い」
"For her body I would give my Soul"
「彼女の体のために、私は私の魂を捧げます」
"and for her love I would surrender heaven"
「そして彼女の愛のために、私は天国を明け渡す」
"Tell me what I ask of thee"
「わたしがあなたに求めることを教えてください」
"Father I implore thee, let me go in peace"
「父よ、どうか安らかに行かせてください」
"Get away from me! Away!" cried the Priest
「私から離れなさい!「どっか行け!」と司祭は叫びました
"thy lover is lost, and thou shalt be lost with her"
「汝の恋人は失われ、汝も彼女と共に迷子となる」
the Priest gave him no blessing
僧侶は彼に何の祝福も与えなかった
and he drove him from his door
そして、彼は彼を戸口から追い出した

the young Fisherman went down into the market-place
若い漁師は市場に下りて行きました

he walked slowly with his head bowed
彼は頭を下げてゆっくりと歩いていた
he walked like one who is in sorrow
彼は悲しみの中にいる人のように歩んだ
the merchants saw the young Fisherman coming
商人たちは若い漁師が来るのを見ました
and the merchants whispered to each other
商人たちは互いにささやき合った
one of the merchants came forth to meet him
商人の一人が彼に会いに来ました
and he called him by his name
そして、その名で彼を呼んだ
"What hast thou to sell?" he asked him
「お前は何を売らなきゃいけないんだ?」と彼は尋ねました
"I will sell thee my Soul," he answered
「わたしはおまえにわたしの魂を売ろう」と彼は答えた
"I pray thee buy my Soul off me"
「どうか私から私の魂を買ってください」
"because I am weary of it"
「うんざりだから」
"of what use is my Soul to me?"
「わたしの魂は、わたしにとって何の役に立ちますか?」
"I cannot see my Soul"
「自分の魂が見えない」
"I cannot touch my Soul"
「私は自分の魂に触れることができない」
"I do not know my Soul"
「私は自分の魂を知らない」
But the merchants only mocked him
しかし、商人たちは彼を嘲笑うだけでした
"Of what use is a man's Soul to us?"
「人間の魂は、私たちにとって何の役に立ちますか?」
"It is not worth a piece of silver"
「銀貨一枚の価値はない」
"Sell us thy body for slavery"
「奴隷として汝の体を売れ」
"and we will clothe thee in sea-purple"

「そして、わたしたちはあなたに海紫の衣をまとわせよう」
"and we'll put a ring upon thy finger"
「お前の指には指輪をはめよう」
"and we'll make thee the minion of the great Queen"
「お前を偉大なる女王の手下にしてやる」
"but don't talk of the Soul to us"
「しかし、私たちに魂のことを話さないでください」
"because for us a Soul is of no use"
「なぜなら、私たちにとって魂は何の役にも立たないからです」
And the young Fisherman thought to himself
そして、若い漁師は考えました
"How strange a thing this is!"
「なんて不思議なことなんだ!」
"The Priest told me the value of the Soul"
「僧侶が魂の価値を教えてくれた」
"the Soul is worth all the gold in the world"
「魂は世界のすべての金に値する」
"but the merchants say a different thing"
「しかし、商人たちは違うことを言っている」
"the Soul is not worth a piece of silver"
「魂は銀貨の価値がない」
And he went out of the market-place
そして、彼は市場から出て行った
and he went down to the shore of the sea
そして海の岸に下りて行った
and he began to ponder on what he should do
そして、彼は自分が何をすべきかについて考え始めました

The Witch
魔女

At noon he remembered one of his friends
正午、彼は友人の一人を思い出した
his friend was a gatherer of samphire
彼の友人はサンフィアの採集者であった
he had told him of a young Witch
彼は若い魔女のことを彼に話した
this young Witch dwelt in a nearby cave
この若い魔女は近くの洞窟に住んでいました
and she was very cunning in her Witcheries
そして、彼女は魔女の儀式において非常に狡猾でした
the young Fisherman stood up and ran to the cave
若い漁師は立ち上がり、洞窟に走って行きました

By the itching of her palm she knew he was coming
手のひらの痒みで、彼女は彼が来ることを悟った
and she laughed, and let down her red hair
そして娘は笑い、赤い髪を下ろしました
She stood at the opening of the cave
彼女は洞窟の入り口に立っていた
her long red hair flowed around her
彼女の長い赤い髪が彼女の周りを流れていた
and in her hand she had a spray of wild hemlock
そして手には野生のツガのスプレーを持っていました
"What do you lack?" she asked, as he came
「何が足りないの?」彼がやって来ると、彼女は尋ねた
he was panting when got to her
彼は彼女に着いたとき、喘いでいた
and he bent down before her
そして彼は彼女の前にかがんだ
"Do you want fish for when there is no wind?"
「風がないときに魚が欲しいの?」
"I have a little reed-pipe"
「小さな葦笛がある」
"when I blow it the mullet come into the bay"

「私が吹くと、ボラが湾に入ってきます」
"But it has a price, pretty boy"
「でも、値段はあるよ、可愛い子」
"What do you lack?"
「何が足りないの?」

"Do you want a storm to wreck the ships?"
「嵐で船が難破したいですか?」
"It will wash the chests of rich treasure ashore"
「宝宝の宝箱を岸に洗い流す」
"I have more storms than the wind"
「私には風よりも嵐のほうが多い」
"I serve one who is stronger than the wind"
「風よりも強い者に仕える」
"I can send the great galleys to the bottom of the sea"
「大きなガレー船を海の底に沈めることができる」
"with a sieve and a pail of water"
「ふるいと水の入ったバケツで」
"But I have a price, pretty boy"
「でも、値段はあるよ、可愛い子」
"What do you lack?"
「何が足りないの?」

"I know a flower that grows in the valley"
「谷間に咲く花を知っている」
"no one knows of this flower, but I"
「この花のことは誰も知らないが、私は」
"this secret flower has purple leaves"
「この秘密の花は紫の葉がついている」
"and in the heart of the flower is a star"
「そして、花の中心には星がある」
"and its juice is as white as milk"
「そして、その果汁は牛乳のように白い」
"touch the lips of the Queen with it"
「それで女王の唇に触れてください」
"and she will follow thee all over the world"
「そうすれば、彼女は世界中であなたに従うでしょう」

"Out of the bed of the King she would rise"
「王様の寝台から起き上がる」
"and over the whole world she would follow thee"
「そして、全世界で、彼女はあなたに従うでしょう」
"But it has a price, pretty boy"
「でも、値段はあるよ、可愛い子」
"What do you lack?"
「何が足りないの?」

"I can pound a toad in a mortar"
「ヒキガエルをすり鉢で叩くことができる」
"and I can make broth of the toad"
「ヒキガエルのスープも作れる」
"stir the broth with a dead man's hand"
「死んだ男の手でスープをかき混ぜる」
"Sprinkle it on thine enemy while he sleeps"
「敵が眠っている間に振りかけろ」
"and he will turn into a black viper"
「そして彼は黒い毒蛇に変わるだろう」
"and his own mother will slay him"
「そして、彼自身の母親が彼を殺すだろう」
"With a wheel I can draw the Moon from heaven"
「車輪で天から月を描ける」
"and in a crystal I can show thee Death"
「そして、水晶の中で、私はあなたに死を示すことができます」
"What do you lack?"
「何が足りないの?」
"Tell me thy desire and I will give it to you"
「あなたの望みを私に伝えてください。そうすれば、私はあなたにそれを与えます」
"and thou shalt pay me a price, pretty boy"
「そして、お前は私に代償を払わなければならない、可愛い子よ」

"My desire is but for a little thing"
「私の望みは、ほんの少しのことだけ」

"yet the Priest was angry with me"
「それなのに、司祭は私に怒った」
"and he chased me away in anger"
「そして彼は怒りに任せて私を追い払った」
"My wish is but for a little thing"
「私の願いは、ほんの少しのことだけ」
"yet the merchants have mocked me"
「それなのに、商人たちは私を嘲笑した」
"and they denied me my wish"
「そして、彼らは私の願いを叶えませんでした」
"Therefore have I come to thee"
「それゆえ、わたしはあなたのところに来たのです」
"I came although men call thee evil"
「わたしは来たが、人々はあなたを悪と呼ぶ」
"but whatever thy price is I shall pay it"
しかし、あなたの代価が何であれ、私はそれを支払います。
"What would'st thou?" asked the Witch
「どうする?」と魔女は尋ねました
and she came near to the Fisherman
そして彼女は漁師に近づきました
"I wish to send my Soul away from me"
「私の魂を私から遠ざけたい」
The Witch grew pale, and shuddered
魔女は青ざめ、身震いしました
and she hid her face in her blue mantle
そして青い外套で顔を隠した
"Pretty boy, that is a terrible thing to do"
「可愛い子、それはひどいことだよ」
He tossed his brown curls and laughed
彼は茶色のカールを揺らして笑った
"My Soul is nought to me" he answered
「私の魂は私には関係ありません」と彼は答えました
"I cannot see my Soul"
「自分の魂が見えない」
"I cannot touch my Soul"
「私は自分の魂に触れることができない」
"I do not know my Soul"

「私は自分の魂を知らない」
the young Witch saw an opportunity
若き魔女は好機を見出しました
"What would thou give me if I tell thee?"
「わたしがあなたに言ったら、あなたはわたしに何をくれるでしょうか?」
and she looked down at him with her beautiful eyes
そして彼女は美しい目で彼を見下ろした
"I will give thee five pieces of gold" he said
「金貨を五枚あげよう」と彼は言いました
"and I will give thee my nets for fishing"
「わたしはあなたに漁用の網をあげよう」
"and I will give thee the house where I live"
「わたしの住む家をあなたに与えよう」
"and you can have my boat"
「そして、あなたは私のボートを持つことができます」
"I will give thee all that I possess"
「わたしの持ち物をすべてあなたにあげよう」
"Tell me how to get rid of my Soul"
「私の魂を取り除く方法を教えて」
She laughed mockingly at him
彼女は彼を嘲るように笑った
and she struck him with the spray of hemlock
そして彼女はツガのスプレーで彼を打った
"I can turn the autumn leaves into gold"
「紅葉を金色に変えられる」
"and I can weave the pale moonbeams into silver"
「そして、私は淡い月光を銀に織り込むことができる」
"He whom I serve is richer than all kings"
「わたしが仕える者は、すべての王よりも富んでいる」
"thy price be neither gold nor silver," he confirmed
「汝の代価は金でも銀でもない」と彼は確認した
"What then shall I give thee if?"
「では、もしおまえに何をあげようか」
"The Witch stroked his hair with her thin white hand"
「魔女は細い白い手で彼の髪を撫でた」
"Thou must dance with me, pretty boy," she murmured

「私と踊らなきゃダメよ、可愛い子」彼女は呟いた
and she smiled at him as she spoke
そして、彼女は話しながら彼に微笑みかけた
"Nothing but that?" cried the young Fisherman
「それ以外は何もないのか?」若い漁師が叫びました
and he wondered why she didn't ask for more
そして、なぜ彼女がもっと求めなかったのか不思議に思いました
"Nothing but that" she answered
「それ以外は」彼女は答えた
and she smiled at him again
そして彼女は再び彼に微笑みかけた
"Then at sunset we shall dance together"
「じゃあ、夕暮れ時に一緒に踊ろう」
"And after we have danced thou shalt tell me"
「そして、私たちが踊った後、あなたは私に言うでしょう」
"The thing which I desire to know"
「知りたいこと」
the young Witch shook her head
若い魔女はかぶりを振った
"When the moon is full" she muttered
「月が満ちたら」と彼女は呟いた
Then she peered all round, and listened
それから辺りを見回し、耳を澄ました
A blue bird rose screaming from its nest
巣から叫ぶ青い鳥が薔薇
and the blue bird circled over the dunes
青い鳥が砂丘の上を旋回した
and three spotted birds rustled in the grass
そして、3羽の斑点のある鳥が草むらでざわめいた
and the birds whistled to each other
鳥たちは互いに口笛を吹いた
There was no other sound except for the sound of a wave
波の音以外、音はなかった
the wave was crushing pebbles
波は小石を砕いていた
So she reached out her hand

だから彼女は手を差し伸べた
and she drew him near to her
そして彼女は彼を自分の方に引き寄せた
and she put her dry lips close to his ear
そして、乾いた唇を彼の耳に近づけた
"Tonight thou must come to the top of the mountain"
「今夜、汝は山の頂上に来なければならない」
"It is a Sabbath, and He will be there"
「それは安息日であり、主はそこにおられる」
The young Fisherman was startled by what she said
若い漁師は彼女の言葉に驚きました
she showed him her white teeth and laughed
彼女は白い歯を見せて笑った
"Who is He of whom thou speakest?"
「あなたが語る方とは、だれですか?」
"It matters not," she answered
「そんなことはどうでもいいわ」彼女は答えた
"Go there tonight," she told him
「今夜、そこへ行きなさい」彼女は彼に言った
"wait for me under the branches of the hornbeam"
「シデの枝の下で待ってて」
"If a black dog runs towards thee don't panic"
「黒い犬が走ってきても慌てるな」
"strike the dog with willow and it will go away"
「柳で犬を叩けば消える」
"If an owl speaks to thee don't answer it"
「フクロウがあなたに話しかけても、それに答えるな」
"When the moon is full I shall be with thee"
「月が満ちるとき、わたしはあなたと共にいる」
"and we will dance together on the grass"
「そして、芝生の上で一緒に踊ろう」
the young Fisherman agreed to do as she said
若い漁師は、彼女の言うとおりにすることに同意しました
"But do you swear to tell me how to send my Soul away?"
「しかし、私の魂を送り出す方法を教えてくれると誓いますか?」
She moved out into the sunlight

彼女は太陽の光の中へと移動した
and the wind rippled through her red hair
そして風が彼女の赤い髪をなびかせた
"By the hoofs of the goat I swear it"
「山羊の蹄によって誓う」
"Thou art the best of the Witches" cried the young Fisherman
「お前は魔女の中で一番だ」と若い漁師は叫びました
"and I will surely dance with thee tonight"
「今夜はきっとあなたと踊ろう」
"I would have preferred it if you had asked for gold"
「金をくれればよかったのに」
"But if this is thy price I shall pay it"
「しかし、これがあなたの代価であるなら、私はそれを支払うでしょう」
"because it is but a little thing"
「それはほんの些細なことだから」
He doffed his cap to her and bent his head low
彼は帽子を脱ぎ捨て、頭を低く下げた
and he ran back to town with joy in his heart
そして、心の中で喜びを胸に町に走って帰りました
And the Witch watched him as he went
そして、魔女は彼が行くのを見ました
when he had passed from her sight she entered her cave
男が彼女の視界から去ったとき、彼女は洞窟に入りました
she took out a mirror from a box
彼女は箱から鏡を取り出した
and she set up the mirror on a frame
そして、鏡をフレームにセットしました
She burned vervain on lighted charcoal before the mirror
彼女は鏡の前で火のついた木炭でクマツヅラを燃やした
and she peered through the coils of the smoke
そして彼女は煙の渦を覗き込んだ
after a time she clenched her hands in anger
しばらくして、彼女は怒りに手を握りしめた
"He should have been mine," she muttered
「あの子は私のものだったはずなのに」 彼女は呟いた
"I am as beautiful as she is"

「私は彼女と同じくらい美しい」

When the moon had risen he left his hut
月が昇ると、男は小屋を出ました
the young Fisherman climbed up to the top of the mountain
若い漁師は山の頂上に登りました
and he stood under the branches of the hornbeam
そして、シデの枝の下に立っていた
The sea lay at his feet like a disc of polished metal
海は彼の足元に、磨かれた金属の円盤のように横たわっていた
the shadows of the fishing boats moved in the little bay
漁船の影が小さな湾を動いた
A great owl with yellow eyes called him
黄色い目をした大きなフクロウが彼を呼んだ
it called him by his name
それは彼を彼の名前で呼んだ
but he made the owl no answer
しかし、彼はフクロウに答えをしませんでした
A black dog ran towards him and snarled
黒い犬が駆け寄ってきて、唸り声を上げた
but he did not panic when the dog came
しかし、犬が来ても慌てませんでした
he struck the dog with a rod of willow
彼は柳の棒で犬を打った
and the dog went away, whining
犬は泣き言を言いながら去っていきました

At midnight the Witches came flying through the air
真夜中、魔女が空を飛んできました
they were like bats flying in the air
まるで空を飛ぶコウモリのようだった
"Phew!" they cried, as they landed on the ground
「ふぅ!」と叫びながら、彼らは地面に着地した
"there is someone here that we don't know!"
「知らない人がいる!」
and they sniffed around for the stranger

そして、見知らぬ人の匂いを嗅ぎまわった
they chattered to each other and made signs
彼らはお互いにおしゃべりをし、合図をしました
Last of all came the young Witch
最後に現れたのは、若い魔女でした
her red hair was streaming in the wind
赤い髪が風になびいていた
She wore a dress of gold tissue
彼女は金のティッシュのドレスを着ていました
and her dress was embroidered with peacocks' eyes
ドレスには孔雀の瞳が刺繍されていた
a little cap of green velvet was on her head
緑色のベルベットの小さな帽子が頭にかかっていた
"Who is he?" shrieked the Witches when they saw her
「あいつは誰だ?」魔女たちは彼女を見て叫びました
but she only laughed, and ran to the hornbeam
しかし、彼女は笑うだけで、シデのところに走った
and she took the Fisherman by the hand
そして漁師の手を取りました
she led him out into the moonlight
彼女は彼を月明かりの中へと連れ出した
and in the moonlight they began to dance
そして月明かりの中、二人は踊り始めた
Round and round they whirled in their dance
ぐるぐる回って踊りながら
she jumped higher and higher into the air
彼女はどんどん高く空中に飛び上がった
he could see the scarlet heels of her shoes
靴の緋色のかかとが見えた
Then came the sound of the galloping of a horse
その時、馬の疾走音が聞こえてきた
but there was no horse to be seen
しかし、馬の姿は見当たらない
and he felt afraid, but he did not know why
そして、彼は恐れを感じたが、その理由はわからなかった
"Faster," cried the Witch to him
「もっと早く」と魔女は叫びました

and she threw her arms around his neck
そして彼女は彼の首に腕を回した
and her breath was hot upon his face
そして彼女の息は彼の顔に熱かった
"Faster, faster!" she cried again
「もっと早く、もっと速く!」彼女は再び叫んだ
the earth seemed to spin beneath his feet
足元で大地が回転しているように見えた
and his thoughts grew more and more troubled
そして、彼の考えはますます悩まされていった
out of nowhere a great terror fell on him
どこからともなく、大きな恐怖が彼に降りかかった
he felt some evil thing was watching him
何か邪悪なものが自分を見ているのを感じた
and at last he became aware of something
そしてとうとう彼は何かに気づいた
under the shadow of a rock there was a figure
岩の影の下に人影があった
a figure that he had not been there before
それまでそこにいなかった姿
It was a man dressed in a black velvet suit
黒いベルベットのスーツを着た男だった
it was styled in the Spanish fashion
スペイン風にスタイリングされていました
the strangers face was strangely pale
見知らぬ男の顔は妙に青ざめていた
but his lips were like a proud red flower
しかし、その唇は誇らしげな赤い花のようだった
He seemed weary of what he was seeing
彼は自分が見ているものにうんざりしているようだった
he was leaning back toying in a listless manner
彼は身を乗り出し、物憂げな態度でもてあそんでいた
he was toying with the pommel of his dagger
彼は短剣の柄頭をもてあそんでいた
on the grass beside him lay a plumed hat
傍らの草の上には羽飾りのついた帽子が置かれていた
and there were a pair of riding gloves with gilt lace

そして、金箔のレースがついた乗馬用手袋もありました
they were sewn with seed-pearls
それらは種真珠で縫い付けられていました
A short cloak lined with sables hung from his shoulder
セーブルで裏打ちされた短いマントが肩からぶら下がっていた

and his delicate white hands were gemmed with rings
そして、彼の繊細な白い手には指輪がはめられていました
Heavy eyelids drooped over his eyes
重い瞼が目の上に垂れ下がった
The young Fisherman watched the stranger
若い漁師は見知らぬ男を見つめていた
just like when one is snared in a spell
呪文に囚われたときのように
At last the Fisherman's and the stranger's eyes met
とうとう漁師と見知らぬ男の目が合った
wherever he danced the eyes seemed to be on him
どこを踊っても、視線が彼に注がれているようだった
He heard the Witch laugh wildly
魔女が荒々しく笑うのが聞こえた
and he caught her by the waist
そして彼は彼女の腰を掴んだ
and he whirled her madly round and round
そして、彼は彼女を狂ったようにぐるぐる回しました
Suddenly a dog barked in the woods
突然、森の中で犬が吠えました
and all the dancers stopped dancing
そして、踊り子たちはみんな踊るのをやめました
they knelt down and kissed the man's hands
二人はひざまずき、男の手にキスをした
As they did so a little smile touched his proud lips
そうしているうちに、誇らしげな唇に小さな笑みが浮かんだ
like when a bird's wing touches the water
鳥の羽が水に触れるときのように
and it makes the water laugh a little
そして、それは水を少し笑わせます
But there was disdain in his smile

しかし、その微笑みには軽蔑が宿っていた
He kept looking at the young Fisherman
彼は若い漁師を見つめ続けた
"Come! let us worship" whispered the Witch
「来い!崇拝しましょう」と魔女はささやきました
and she led him up to the man
そして、彼女は彼を男のところに連れて行きました
a great desire to follow her seized him
彼女を追いかけたいという大きな願望が彼を捕らえました
and he followed her to the man
そして、男のところまでついて行きました
But when he came close he made the sign of the Cross
しかし、イエスが近づいたとき、十字架のしるしをなさった
he did this without knowing why he did it
彼はなぜそんなことをしたのかも知らずに、こんなことをしたのです
and he called upon the holy name
そして彼は聖なる御名を呼び求めた
As soon as he did this the Witches screamed like hawks
彼がそうするやいなや、魔女たちは鷹のように叫びました
and all the Witches flew away like bats
そして、すべての魔女はコウモリのように飛び去りました
the figure under the shadow tWitched with pain
影の下の人影は苦痛に痙攣した
The man went over to a little wood and whistled
男は小さな森のところへ行き、口笛を吹きました
A horse with silver trappings came running to meet him
銀の飾りをつけた馬が走ってきて、彼を迎えに来ました
As he leapt upon the saddle he turned round
鞍に飛び乗ると、彼は振り返った
and he looked at the young Fisherman sadly
そして、悲しそうに若い漁師を見ました
the Witch with the red hair also tried to fly away
赤い髪の魔女も飛び去ろうとしました
but the Fisherman caught her by her wrists
しかし、漁師は彼女の手首をつかみました
and he kept hold of her tightly

そして彼は彼女をしっかりと抱きしめ続けた
"Let me loose!" she cried, "Let me go!"
「放して!」と彼女は叫びました。
"thou hast named what should not be named"
「あなたは名付けてはならないものに名前を付けた」
"and thou hast shown the sign that may not be looked at"
「そして、あなたは見てはいけないしるしを示しました」
"I will not let thee go till thou hast told me the secret"
「お前が秘密を話すまで、俺はお前を逃がさない」
"What secret?" said the Witch
「どんな秘密?」と魔女は言いました
and she wrestled with him like a wild cat
そして、彼女は野良猫のように彼と格闘した
and she bit her foam-flecked lips
そして彼女は泡だらけの唇を噛んだ
"You know the secret," replied the Fisherman
「秘密知ってるだろ」と漁師は答えました
Her grass-green eyes grew dim with tears
草緑の瞳は涙でぼんやりとしていた
"Ask me anything but that!" she begged of the Fisherman
「それ以外は何でも聞いて!」と漁師に懇願しました
He laughed, and held her all the more tightly
彼は笑い、彼女をいっそう強く抱きしめた
She saw that she could not free herself
彼女は自分を解放できないことを悟った
when she realized this she whispered to him
それに気づいたとき、彼女は彼にささやいた
"Surely I am as fair as the daughters of the sea"
「確かに私は海の娘のように公平です」
"and I am as comely as those that dwell in the blue waters"
「わたしは青い海に住む者のように美しい」
and she fawned on him and put her face close to his
そして、娘は彼に媚びへつらい、彼の顔に顔を近づけました
But he thrust her back and replied to her
しかし、彼は彼女を突き飛ばし、彼女に返事をしました
"If thou don't keep your promise I will slay thee"
「約束を守らなければ、お前を殺す」

"I will slay thee for a false Witch"
「偽りの魔女のためにお前を殺してやる」
She grew gas rey as a blossom of the Judas tree
彼女はユダの木の花のようにガスレイを育てた
and a strange shudder past through her body
そして奇妙な震えが彼女の体を駆け巡った
"if that is how you want it to be," she muttered
「そうありたいのなら」彼女は呟いた
"It is thy Soul and not mine"
「それはあなたの魂であり、私の魂ではありません」
"Do with your Soul as thou wish"
「汝の望むように、あなたの魂を働かせなさい」
And she took from her girdle a little knife
そして、帯から小さなナイフを取り出しました
the knife had a handle of green viper's skin
ナイフには緑色の毒蛇の皮の柄が付いていた
and she gave him this green little knife
そして、この緑色の小さなナイフを彼に与えました
"What shall I do with this?" he asked of her
「これをどうしようか？」と彼は彼女に尋ねた
She was silent for a few moments
彼女はしばし沈黙した
a look of terror came over her face
彼女の顔に恐怖の表情が浮かんだ
Then she brushed her hair back from her forehead
それから彼女は額から髪をかき上げた
and, smiling strangely, she spoke to him
そして、不思議な笑みを浮かべて、彼に話しかけた
"men call it the shadow of the body"
「男性はそれを身体の影と呼ぶ」
"but it is not the shadow of the body"
「しかし、それは身体の影ではない」
"the shadow is the body of the Soul"
「影は魂の体である」
"Stand on the sea-shore with thy back to the moon"
「月に背を向けて海岸に立つ」
"cut away from around thy feet thy shadow"

「汝の足のまわりを断ち切れ、汝の影」
"the shadow, which is thy Soul's body"
「汝の魂の体である影」
"and bid thy Soul to leave thee"
「そして、あなたの魂にあなたから離れるように命じてください」
"and thy Soul will leave thee"
「そうすれば、あなたの魂はあなたから離れる」
The young Fisherman trembled, "Is this true?"
若い漁師は「本当ですか?」と震えました。
"what I have said is true," she answered him
「私が言ったことは本当です」と彼女は彼に答えました
"and I wish that I had not told thee of it"
「おまえに言わなければよかったのに」
she cried, and clung to his knees weeping
彼女は泣き叫び、膝にしがみついて泣いた
he moved her away from him in the tall grass
彼は背の高い草むらで彼女を彼から遠ざけた
and he placed the little green knife in his belt
そして、小さな緑色のナイフをベルトに入れました
then he went to the edge of the mountain
それから山のはずれに行きました
from the edge of the mountain he began to climb down
山の端から、彼は下り始めました

The Soul
魂

his Soul called out to him
彼の魂は彼に呼びかけた
"I have dwelt with thee for all these years"
「わたしは、この数年間、あなたと共に住んできた」
"and I have been thy servant"
「わたしはあなたのしもべでした」
"Don't send me away from thee"
「私をあなたから遠ざけないでください」
"what evil have I done thee?"
「わたしはあなたにどんな悪事を働いたのか」。
And the young Fisherman laughed
そして若い漁師は笑った
"Thou has done me no evil"
「あなたは私に悪をなさらなかった」
"but I have no need of thee"
「しかし、わたしはあなたを必要としません」
"The world is wide"
「世界は広い」
"there is Heaven and Hell in this life"
「この世には天国と地獄がある」
"and there a dim twilight between them"
「そして、二人の間には薄暗い黄昏が広がっている」
"Go wherever thou wilt, but trouble me not"
どこへでも行きなさい。しかし、私を困らせてはならない
"because my love is calling to me"
「私の愛が私を呼んでいるから」
His Soul besought him piteously
彼の魂は哀れに彼に懇願した
but the young Fisherman heeded it not
しかし、若いフィッシュマーマンはそれに耳を貸さなかった
instead, he leapt from crag to crag
代わりに、彼は岩山から岩山へと飛び移った
he moved as sure-footed as a wild goat
彼は野生のヤギのように確かな足取りで動いた

and at last he reached the level ground
そして、とうとう平地にたどり着いた
and then he reached the yellow shore of the sea
そして、黄色い海の岸辺に着きました
He stood on the sand with his back to the moon
彼は月に背を向けて砂の上に立っていた
and out of the sea-foam came white arms
そして、海の泡から白い腕が出てきた
the arms of the mermaid beckoned him to come
人魚の腕が彼を手招きした
Before him lay his shadow; the body of his Soul
彼の前には彼の影が横たわっていた。彼の魂の体
behind him hung the moon, in honey-coloured air
彼の背後には、蜂蜜色の空気を漂わせた月が浮かんでいた
And his Soul spoke to him again
そして彼の魂は再び彼に語りかけた
"thou hast decided to drive me away from thee"
「あなたは私をあなたから追い払うことに決めた」
"but send me not forth without a heart"
「しかし、心のない私を送り出さないでください」
"The world you are sending me to is cruel"
「あなたが私を送り込んでいる世界は残酷です」
"give me thy heart to take with me"
「あなたの心を私に与えてください」
He tossed his head and smiled
彼は首をかしげて微笑んだ
"With what should I love if I gave thee my heart?"
「わたしがあなたにわたしの心を捧げたら、わたしは何を愛せばよいのか」
"Nay, but be merciful," said his Soul
「いや、だが憐れみ深くあれ」と彼の魂は言った
"give me thy heart, for the world is very cruel"
あなたの心を私に与えてください。世界はとても残酷です
"and I am afraid," begged his soul
「そして、私は恐れている」と彼の魂に懇願した
"My heart belongs my love," he answered
「私の心は私の愛のものです」と彼は答えました

"Should I not love also?" asked his Soul
「私も愛すべきではないのか?」と彼の魂は尋ねた
but the fisherman didn't answer his soul
しかし、漁師は彼の魂に答えませんでした
"Get thee gone, for I have no need of thee"
「お前を去らせろ、お前なんかいらないから」
and he took the little knife
そして、彼は小さなナイフを取りました
the knife with its handle of green viper's skin
緑色の毒蛇の皮の柄が付いたナイフ
and he cut away his shadow from around his feet
そして、足の周りの影を切り落とした
and his shadow rose up and stood before him
すると、彼の影が立ち上がり、彼の前に立ちはだかった
his shadow was just like he was
彼の影は、まさに彼と同じだった
and his shadow looked just like he did
そして、彼の影は彼と同じように見えました
He crept back and put his knife into his belt
彼は忍び寄り、ナイフをベルトに差し込んだ
A feeling of awe came over him
畏敬の念が彼を襲った
"Get thee gone," he murmured
「さっさと行け」彼は呟いた
"let me see thy face no more"
「もうあなたの顔を見させないで」
"Nay, but we must meet again," said the Soul
「いや、でもまた会わなきゃいけない」と魂は言いました
His Soul's voice was low and like a flute
彼の魂の声は低く、フルートのようでした
its lips hardly moved while it spoke
喋っている間、その唇はほとんど動かなかった
"How shall we meet?" asked the young Fisherman
「どうやって会おうか?」と若い漁師は尋ねました
"Thou wilt not follow me into the depths of the sea?"
「お前は私を追って海の深みに入らないのか?」
"Once every year I will come to this place"

「年に一度、この場所に来る」
"I will call to thee," said the Soul
「わたしは汝を呼ぶ」と魂は言った
"It may be that thou will have need of me"
「汝は私を必要としているかも知れない」
the young Fishermam did not see a reason
若いフィッシャーマムは理由がわからなかった
"What need could I have of thee?"
「わたしがあなたに何の用があるというのですか?」
"but be it as thou wilt"
「しかし、あなたの御心にかなうように」
he plunged into the deep dark waters
彼は深く暗い海に飛び込んだ
and the Tritons blew their horns to welcome him
トリトンは角笛を吹いて彼を歓迎した
the little Mermaid rose up to meet her lover
人魚姫は恋人に会うために立ち上がりました
she put her arms around his neck
彼女は彼の首に腕を回した
and she kissed him on the mouth
そして彼女は彼の口にキスをした
His Soul stood on the lonely beach
彼の魂は孤独な浜辺に立っていた
his Soul watched them sink into the sea
彼の魂は、彼らが海に沈むのを見ていた
then his Soul went weeping away over the marshes
それから彼の魂は沼地の向こうで泣きながら去っていきました

After the First Year
1年目以降

it had been one year since had he cast his soul away
彼が魂を捨ててから1年が経っていた
the Soul came back to the shore of the sea
魂は海の岸に帰ってきた
and the Soul called to the young Fisherman
そして魂は若い漁師に呼ばれました
the young Fisherman rose back out of the sea
若い漁師は海から上がりました
he asked his soul, "Why dost thou call me?"
彼は魂に尋ねた、「なぜ私を呼んだのですか」。
And the Soul answered, "Come nearer"
すると魂は「もっと近づいてきなさい」と答えた
"come nearer, so that I may speak with thee"
「わたしがあなたと話すために、もっと近づいてきなさい」
"I have seen marvellous things"
「私は素晴らしいものを見てきました」
So the young Fisherman came nearer to his soul
それで、若い漁師は彼の魂に近づきました
and he couched in the shallow water
そして彼は浅瀬に身を潜めた
and he leaned his head upon his hand
そして、その手に頭をもたせかけた
and he listened to his Soul
そして彼は自分の魂に耳を傾けた
and his Soul spoke to him
そして彼の魂は彼に語りかけた

When I left thee I turned East
歌詞の意味:
私はあなたを去ったとき、私は東に向きを変えました。
From the East cometh everything that is wise
東から知恵あるものはすべて来る
For six days I journeyed eastwards
6日間、私は東方へ旅をした

on the morning of the seventh day I came to a hill
七日目の朝、わたしは丘に来ました
a hill that is in the country of the Tartars
タルタール人の国にある丘
I sat down under the shade of a tamarisk tree
私はタマリスクの木陰に腰を下ろした
in order to shelter myself from the sun
太陽から身を守るために
The land was dry and had burnt up from the heat
大地は乾燥し、暑さで燃え尽きていた
The people went to and fro over the plain
人々は平原を行ったり来たりした
they were like flies crawling on polished copper
磨かれた銅の上を這う蝿のようだった
When it was noon a cloud of red dust rose
正午になると、赤い砂埃の雲が立ち上った
When the Tartars saw it they strung their bows
タルタール人はそれを見ると、弓を張った
and they leapt upon their little horses
そして、小さな馬に飛び乗った
they galloped to meet the cloud of red dust
彼らは赤い塵の雲に会うために疾走した
The women fled to the wagons, screamin
女たちは叫びながら荷馬車に逃げ込んだ
they hid themselves behind the felt curtains
彼らはフェルトのカーテンの後ろに身を隠した
At twilight the Tartars returned to their camp
黄昏時、タルタール人は野営地に戻った
but five of them did not return
しかし、そのうちの5人は戻ってこなかった
many of them had been wounded
彼らの多くが負傷していた
They harnessed their horses to the wagons
彼らは馬を荷馬車に繋ぎ着かせた
and they drove away hastily
そして、彼らは急いで走り去った
Three jackals came out of a cave and peered after them

3匹のジャッカルが洞窟から出てきて、彼らの後を覗き込んだ
the jackals sniffed the air with their nostrils
ジャッカルは鼻孔で空気の匂いを嗅いだ
and they trotted off in the opposite direction
そして、彼らは反対方向に小走りで走り去りました
When the moon rose I saw a camp-fire
月が昇ると、焚き火が見えた
and I went towards the fire in the distance
そして、私は遠くの火の方へ行きました
A company of merchants were seated round the fire
商人の一団が火を囲んで座っていた
the merchants were sitting on their carpets
商人たちは絨毯の上に座っていた
Their camels were tied up behind them
彼らのラクダは彼らの後ろに縛り付けられていました
and their servants were pitching tents in the sand
しもべたちは砂の中に天幕を張っていた
As I came near them the chief rose up
私が彼らに近づくと、酋長が立ち上がった
he drew his sword and asked me my intentions
彼は剣を抜き、私の意図を尋ねた
I answered that I was a Prince in my own land
私は自分の国の王子様だと答えました
I said I had escaped from the Tartars
私はタルタール人から逃げたと言った
they had sought to make me their slave
彼らは私を奴隷にしようとしました
The chief smiled and showed me five heads
村長はにっこりと微笑み、5つの頭を私に見せてくれた
the heads were fixed upon long reeds of bamboo
頭は長い竹の葦に固定されていた
Then he asked me who was the prophet of God
それから彼は私に、神の預言者はだれかと尋ねました
I answered him that it was, "Mohammed"
私は彼に「モハメッド」と答えました
He bowed and took me by the hand
彼はお辞儀をして、私の手を取った

and he let me sit by his side
そして、彼は私を彼のそばに座らせてくれました
A servant brought me some mare's milk in a wooden-dish
召使いが木の皿に入った牝馬のミルクを持ってきてくれた
and he brought a piece of lamb's flesh
そして、小羊の肉の切れ端を持って来た
At daybreak we started on our journey
夜明けとともに、私たちは旅を始めました
I rode on a red-haired camel, by the side of the chief
私は赤毛のラクダに乗って、酋長のそばを通りました
a runner ran before us, carrying a spear
槍を持ったランナーが私たちの前を走った
The men of war were on both sides of us
戦争の男たちは私たちの両側にいました
and the mules followed with the merchandise
そして、ラバは商品を持って続きました
There were forty camels in the caravan
キャラバンには40頭のラクダがいました
and the mules were twice forty in number
ラバは四十頭の二倍であった

We went from the land of Tartars to the land of Gryphons
私たちはタルタル人の地からグリフォンの地に行きました
The folk of the Gryphons curse the Moon
グリフォンの民は月を呪う
We saw the Gryphons on the white rocks
白い岩の上にグリフォンが見えました
they were guarding their gold treasure
彼らは金の宝を守っていた
And we saw the scaled Dragons sleeping in their caves
そして、鱗のあるドラゴンが洞窟で眠っているのを見ました
As we passed over the mountains we held our breath
山を越えるとき、私たちは息を止めました
so that the snow would not fall on us
雪が降らないように
and each man tied a veil over his eyes
そして、男はおのおの、その目を覆うベールを結んだ

when we passed through the valleys of the Pygmies
ピグミーの渓谷を通り抜けた時
and the Pygmies shot their arrows at us
ピグミー族は我々に矢を放った
they shot from the hollows of the trees
彼らは木々の窪みから撃った
at night we heard the wild men beat their drums
夜になると、野生の男たちが太鼓を叩くのが聞こえました
When we came to the Tower of Apes we offered fruits
猿の塔に来たとき、私たちは果物を捧げました
and those inthe tower of the Apes did not harm us
猿の塔にいた者たちは、我々に危害を加えなかった
When we came to the Tower of Serpents we offered milk
蛇の塔に来たとき、私たちはミルクを捧げました
and those in the tower of the Serpents let us go past
そして、蛇の塔にいる者たちは、私たちを通り過ぎさせてください
Three times in our journey we came to the banks of the Oxus
旅の途中で3回、オクサス川のほとりに来ました
We crossed the river Oxus on rafts of wood
私たちは木の筏でオクサス川を渡りました
The river horses raged and tried to slay us
川の馬は激怒し、私たちを殺そうとしました
When the camels saw them they trembled
ラクダはそれを見ると震え上がりました
The kings of each city levied tolls on us
各都市の王たちは、私たちに通行料を課しました
but they would not allow us to enter their gates
しかし、彼らは私たちが彼らの門に入ることを許しませんでした
They threw bread over the walls to us
彼らは壁越しにパンを投げつけました
and they gave us little maize-cakes baked in honey
そして、蜂蜜で焼いた小さなトウモロコシのケーキをくれました
and cakes of fine flour filled with dates
ナツメヤシを詰めた上質な小麦粉のケーキ

For every hundred baskets we gave them a bead of amber
籠100個ごとに琥珀のビーズをあげました
When villagers saw us coming they poisoned the wells
村人たちは私たちが来るのを見ると、井戸に毒を盛った
and the villagers fled to the hill-summits
村人たちは丘の頂上に逃げた
on our journey we fought with the Magadae
旅の途中、私たちはマガダエ族と戦った
They are born old, and grow younger every year
彼らは年老いて生まれ、毎年若返ります
they die when they are little children
彼らは幼い頃に死んでしまいます
and on our journey we fought with the Laktroi
そして旅の途中でラクトロイと戦った
they say that the Laktroi are the sons of tigers
ラクトロイ族は虎の息子だと言われている
and they paint themselves yellow and black
そして、彼らは自分自身を黄色と黒に塗ります
And on our journey we fought with the Aurantes
そして旅の途中で、私たちはアウランテスと戦いました
they bury their dead on the tops of trees
彼らは死者を木のてっぺんに埋葬します
the Sun, who is their god, slays their buried
彼らの神である太陽は、彼らの埋葬された人々を殺します
so they live in dark caverns
だから彼らは暗い洞窟に住んでいます
And on our journey we fought with the Krimnians
そして旅の途中で、私たちはクリムニア人と戦った
the folk of the Krimnians worship a crocodile
クリムニアの民はワニを崇拝している
they give the crocodile earrings of green glass
彼らは緑色のガラスのクロコダイルイヤリングを与えます
they feed the crocodile with butter and fresh fowls
彼らはワニにバターと新鮮な家禽を与えます
we fought with the Agazonbae, who are dog-faced
犬の顔をしたアガゾンバエと戦った
and we fought with the Sibans, who have horses' feet

そして、馬の足を持つシバン人と戦った
and they can run swifter than the fastest horses
そして、彼らは最速の馬よりも速く走ることができます

A third of our army died in battle
我が軍の三分の一が戦死した
a third of our army died from want of food
我が軍の三分の一が食糧不足で死んだ
The rest of our army murmured against me
我が軍の残りの者たちは、私に対して呟いた
they said that I had brought them an evil fortune
彼らは、わたしが彼らに邪悪な幸運をもたらしたと言いました
I took an adder from beneath a stone
私は石の下から足し算を取り出しました
and I let the adder bite my hand
そして私は加算器に私の手を噛ませました
When they saw I did not sicken they grew afraid
わたしが病気にならないのを見て、彼らは恐れを募らせた
In the fourth month we reached the city of Illel
4ヶ月目にはイレルの街に着きました
It was night time when we reached the city
街に着いたのは夜でした
we arrived at the grove outside the city walls
城壁の外の木立に着きました
the air in the city was sultry
街の空気は蒸し暑かった
because the Moon was travelling in Scorpion
月が蠍を旅していたから
We took the ripe pomegranates from the trees
熟したザクロを木から取り除きました
and we broke them, and drank their sweet juices
そして、私たちはそれらを壊し、彼らの甘いジュースを飲みました
Then we laid down on our carpets
それから絨毯の上に横になりました
and we waited for the dawn to come

そして夜明けが来るのを待ちました
At dawn we rose and knocked at the gate of the city
夜明けとともに、私たちは立ち上がり、町の門をたたきました

the gate was wrought out of red bronze
門は赤い青銅でできていた

and the gate had carvings of sea-dragons
門には海龍の彫刻があった

The guards looked down from the battlements
衛兵たちは胸壁から見下ろした

and they asked us what our intentions were
そして、彼らは私たちの意図が何であるかを尋ねました

The interpreter of the caravan answered
キャラバンの通訳が答えた

we said we had come from the land of Syria
私たちはシリアの地から来たと言いました

and we told him we had many merchandise
そして、私たちはたくさんの商品を持っていることを彼に伝えました

They took some of us as hostages
彼らは私たちの何人かを人質にしました

and they told us they would open the gate at noon
そして、正午に門を開けると言いました

when it was noon they opened the gate
正午になると、彼らは門を開けた

when we entered the people came out of the houses
私たちが中に入ると、人々は家から出てきました

they came in order to look at us
彼らは私たちを見るためにやって来ました

and a town crier went around the city
そして、町の叫び声が町中を回った

he made announcements of our arrival through a shell
彼は殻を通して私たちの到着を知らせました

We stood in the market-place of the medina
私たちはメディナの市場に立っていました

and the servants uncorded the bales of cloths
しもべたちは布の俵をほどいた

they opened the carved chests of sycamore
彼らはプラタナスの彫刻された箱を開けた
Then merchants set forth their strange wares
それから商人たちは奇妙な品物を並べた
waxed linen from Egypt, painted linen from the Ethiops
エジプト産の蝋引きリネン、エチオピア産の塗装リネン
purple sponges from Tyre, cups of cold amber
ツロの紫色のスポンジ、冷たい琥珀のカップ
fine vessels of glass, and curious vessels of burnt clay
ガラスの細かい器と、焼けた粘土の奇妙な器
From the roof of a house a company of women watched us
一軒の家の屋根から、一団の女性が私たちを見ていた
One of them wore a mask of gilded leather
そのうちの一人は金箔の革の仮面をかぶっていた

on the first day the Priests came and bartered with us
初日、僧侶たちがやってきて、私たちと物々交換をしました
On the second day the nobles came and bartered with us
二日目に貴族たちがやってきて、私たちと物々交換をしました
on the third day the craftsmen came and bartered with us
3日目に職人がやってきて、私たちと物々交換をしました
all of them brought their slaves to us
彼らは皆、奴隷を私たちのところに連れて来ました
this is their custom with all merchants
これはすべての商人の習慣です
we waited for the moon to come
月が来るのを待ちました
when the moon was waning I wandered away
月が傾く頃、私はさまよった
I wondered through the streets of the city
街の通りを不思議に思った
and I came to the garden of the city's God
そして、わたしは町の神の園に着いた
The Priests in their yellow robes moved silently
黄色いローブに身を包んだ僧侶たちは静かに動いた
they moved through the green trees

二人は緑の木々の間を進んだ
There was a pavement of black marble
そこには黒い大理石の舗道があった
and on this pavement stood a rose-red house
そして、この舗道の上には、バラ色の家が立っていました
this was the house in which the God was dwelling
これは神が住まわれていた家でした
its doors were of powdered lacquer
その扉は粉末漆でできていた
and bulls and peacocks were wrought on the doors
また、雄牛と孔雀が戸口に細工されていた
and the doors were polished with gold
扉は金で磨かれていた
The tiled roof was of sea-green porcelain
瓦葺きの屋根は海緑色の磁器でできていた
and the jutting eaves were festooned with little bells
突き出た軒先には小さな鈴が飾られていた
When the white doves flew past they struck the bells
白い鳩が通り過ぎると、鈴を打ちました
they struck the bells with their wings
彼らは翼で鐘を叩いた
and the doves made the bells tinkle
そして鳩は鈴を鳴らしました
In front of the temple was a pool of clear water
寺院の前には澄んだ水が溜まっていました
the pool was paved with veined onyx
プールは縞模様のオニキスで舗装されていました
I laid down beside the water of the pool
私はプールの水辺に横たわった
and with my pale fingers I touched the broad leaves
そして、青白い指で広い葉に触れました
One of the Priests came towards me
僧侶の一人が私の方へ近づいてきた
and the priest stood behind me
そして、司祭は私の後ろに立っていた
He had sandals on his feet
足元にはサンダルを履いていた

one sandal was of soft serpent-skin
一本のサンダルは柔らかい蛇の皮でできていた
and the other sandal was of birds' plumage
もう一本のサンダルは鳥の羽でできていました
On his head was a mitre of black felt
頭には黒いフェルトの留め釘が乗っていた
and it was decorated with silver crescents
そして、それは銀の三日月で飾られていました
Seven kinds of yellow were woven into his robe
彼のローブには7種類の黄色が織り込まれていた
and his frizzed hair was stained with antimony
縮れた髪はアンチモンで汚れていた

After a little while he spoke to me
しばらくして、彼は私に話しかけてきました
finally, he asked me my desire
最後に、彼は私の希望を尋ねました
I told him that my desire was to see their god
私は彼に、私の願いは彼らの神に会いたいと言いました
He looked strangely at me with his small eyes
彼は小さな瞳で不思議そうに私を見つめていた
"The god is hunting," said the Priest
「神は狩りをしている」と司祭は言った
I did not accept the answer of the priest
私は僧侶の答えを受け入れませんでした
"Tell me in what forest and I will ride with him"
「どの森で教えて、一緒に乗る」
his finger nails were long and pointed
彼の指の爪は長く、尖っていた
he combed out the soft fringes of his tunic
彼はチュニックの柔らかな裾を梳いた
"The god is asleep," he murmured
「神は眠っている」彼は呟いた
"Tell me on what couch, and I will watch over him"
「どのソファに座っていたか教えてください。私が彼を見守ってあげます」
"The god is at the feast" he cried

「神は祝宴に出席している」と彼は叫んだ
"If the wine be sweet, I will drink it with him"
「ワインが甘かったら、一緒に飲むよ」
"and if the wine be bitter, I will drink it with him also"
「ぶどう酒が苦いなら、わたしも一緒に飲もう」
He bowed his head in wonder
彼は驚いて頭を下げた
then he took me by the hand
それから彼は私の手を取った
and raised me up onto my feet
そして私を立ち上がらせてくれました
and he led me into the temple
そして、私を神殿に連れて行った

In the first chamber I saw an idol
最初の部屋で私は偶像を見た
This idol was seated on a throne of jasper
この偶像は碧玉の玉座に座っていた
the idol was bordered with great orient pearls
偶像は東洋の大真珠で縁取られていました
and on its forehead was a great ruby
そして、その額には大きなルビーが描かれていました
the idol was of a man, carved out of ebony
偶像は黒檀から彫られた男のものだった
thick oil dripped from its hair to its thighs
髪の毛から太ももまで濃厚なオイルが滴り落ちた
Its feet were red with the blood of a newly-slain lamb
その足は、屠られたばかりの子羊の血で赤くなっていた
and its loins girt with a copper belt
腰には銅の帯が巻かれている
copper that was studded with seven beryls
7つのベリルがちりばめられた銅
And I said to the Priest, "Is this the god?"
そして、私は司祭に言った、「これは神ですか？」
And he answered me, "This is the god"
すると彼は「これが神だ」と答えました
"Show me the god," I cried, "or I will slay thee"

「神を見せてやれ」と私は叫んだ、「さもなくばお前を殺すぞ」

I touched his hand and it withered
私は彼の手に触れ、それは萎えました
"Let my lord heal his servant," he begged me
「我が主君に召使いを癒し給え」と彼は私に懇願した
"heal his servant and I will show him the God"
「彼のしもべをいやしなさい。そうすれば、わたしは彼に神を見せよう」
So I breathed with my breath upon his hand
だから私は彼の手に息を吹きかけた
when I did this his hand became whole again
私がそうすると、彼の手は再び完全になりました
and the priest trembled with fear
祭司は恐怖におののいた
Then he led me into the second chamber
それから彼は私を第二の部屋に連れて行きました
in this chamber I saw another idol
この部屋で、私はもう一人の偶像を見た
The idol was standing on a lotus of jade
偶像は翡翠の蓮の上に立っていた
the lotus hung with great emeralds
蓮は素晴らしいエメラルドで吊るされていました
and the lotus was carved out of ivory
そして、蓮は象牙から彫られた
its stature was twice the stature of a man
その背丈は人間の背丈の2倍でした
On its forehead was a great chrysolite
その額には大きなクリソライトがありました
its breasts were smeared with myrrh and cinnamon
その胸は没薬とシナモンで塗られていた
In one hand it held a crooked sceptre of jade
片手には翡翠の曲がった笏を持っていた
and in the other hand it held a round crystal
そしてもう片方の手には丸い水晶が握られていた
and its thick neck was circled with selenites
そして、その太い首はセレナイトで囲まれていました

I asked the Priest, "Is this the god?"
私は僧侶に「これが神ですか?」と尋ねました。
he answered me, "This is the god"
彼は私に答えた、「これは神です」。
"Show me the god," I cried, "or I will slay thee"
「神を見せてやれ」と私は叫んだ、「さもなくばお前を殺すぞ」
And I touched his eyes and they became blind
わたしが彼の目に触れると、彼らは盲目になった
And the Priest begged me for mercy
そして司祭は私に慈悲を乞いました
"Let my lord heal his servant"
「わが主君に召使いを癒させなさい」
"heal me and I will show him the God"
「私を癒してください。そうすれば、私は彼に神を見せます」
So I breathed with my breath upon his eyes
だから私は彼の目に息を吹きかけた
and the sight came back to his eyes
そして、その光景が彼の目に蘇った
He trembled with fear again
彼は再び恐怖に震えた
and then he led me into the third chamber
そして、彼は私を第三の部屋に連れて行ってくれました

There was no idol in the third chamber
第三の部屋には偶像はなかった
there were no images of any kind
画像は一切ありませんでした
all there was in the room was a mirror
部屋には鏡しかありませんでした
the mirror was made of round metal
鏡は丸い金属でできていました
the mirror was set on an altar of stone
鏡は石の祭壇の上に置かれていた
I said to the Priest, "Where is the god?"
私は司祭に「神はどこにいるのか」と言いました。

he answered me, "There is no god but this mirror
彼は私に答えた、「この鏡以外に神はいない
because this is the Mirror of Wisdom
なぜなら、これは知恵の鏡だからです
It reflects all things that are in heaven
それは天国にあるすべてのものを反映しています
and it reflects all things that are on earth
そして、それは地球上のすべてのものを反映しています
except for the face of him who looketh into it
それを覗き込む者の顔を除いては
him who looketh into it it reflects not
それを覗き込む者は、それを映し出さない
so he who looketh into the mirror will become wise
鏡を覗き込む者は賢くなる
there are many other mirrors in the world
世界には他にもたくさんの鏡があります
but they are mirrors of opinion
しかし、それらは意見の鏡です
This is the only mirror that shows Wisdom
これは知恵を示す唯一の鏡です
those who possess this mirror know everything
この鏡を持っている人は、すべてを知っている
There isn't anything that is hidden from them
彼らから隠されているものは何もありません
And those who don't possess the mirror don't have Wisdom
そして、鏡を持たない者には知恵がない
Therefore this mirror is the God
それゆえ、この鏡は神である
and that is why we worship this mirror
だからこそ、私たちはこの鏡を崇拝するのです
And I looked into the mirror
そして鏡を覗き込んだ
and it was as he had said to me
そして、それは彼が私に言ったとおりでした

And then I did a strange thing
そして、私は奇妙なことをしました

but what I did matters not
しかし、私が何をしたかは重要ではありません
There a valley that is but a day's journey from here
ここから1日しかかからない渓谷がある
in this valley I have hidden the Mirror of Wisdom
この谷に、私は知恵の鏡を隠した
Allow me to enter into thee again
歌詞の意味: 再びあなたの中に入ることを許可します。
accept me and thou shalt be wiser than all the wise men
わたしを受け入れなさい、そうすればあなたはすべての賢者よりも賢くなるでしょう
let me enter into thee and none will be as wise as thou
わたしがあなたの中に入るようにしなさい、そうすればあなたほど賢明な者はいないでしょう
But the young Fisherman laughed
しかし、若い漁師は笑いました
"Love is better than Wisdom"
「愛は知恵にまさる」
"The little Mermaid loves me"
「人魚姫は私を愛している」
"But there is nothing better than Wisdom" said the Soul
「しかし、知恵に勝るものはない」と魂は言いました
"Love is better," answered the young Fisherman
「愛のほうがいいよ」と若い漁師は答えました
and he plunged into the deep sea
そして彼は深海に飛び込んだ
and the Soul went weeping away over the marshes
そして、魂は沼地の上で泣きながら去って行きました

After the Second Year
2年目以降

it had been two years since he had cast his soul away
魂を捨ててから2年が経っていた
the Soul came back to the shore of the sea
魂は海の岸に帰ってきた
and the Soul called to the young Fisherman
そして魂は若い漁師に呼ばれました
the young Fisherman rose back out of the sea
若い漁師は海から上がりました
he asked his soul, "Why dost thou call me?"
彼は魂に尋ねた、「なぜ私を呼んだのですか」。
And the Soul answered, "Come nearer"
すると魂は「もっと近づいてきなさい」と答えた
"come nearer, so that I may speak with thee"
「わたしがあなたと話すために、もっと近づいてきなさい」
"I have seen marvellous things"
「私は素晴らしいものを見てきました」
So the young Fisherman came nearer to his soul
それで、若い漁師は彼の魂に近づきました
and he couched in the shallow water
そして彼は浅瀬に身を潜めた
and he leaned his head upon his hand
そして、その手に頭をもたせかけた
and he listened to his Soul
そして彼は自分の魂に耳を傾けた
and his Soul spoke to him
そして彼の魂は彼に語りかけた

When I left thee I turned my face to the South
汝と別れた時、私は南に顔を向けた
From the South cometh everything that is precious
尊いものはすべて南からやって来る
Six days I journeyed along the dusty paths
埃っぽい道を6日間旅した
and the paths led to the city of Ashter

そして、道はアシュテルの町に通じていた
ways by which the pilgrims are wont to go
巡礼者が通らない道
on the morning of the seventh day I lifted up my eyes
七日目の朝、わたしは目を上げた
and lo! the city of Ashter lay at my feet
そして見よ!アシュターの町が私の足元に横たわっていた
because the city of Ashter is in a valley
アシュテルの町は谷間にあるからです
There are nine gates around this city
この街の周りには9つの門があります
in front of each gate stands a bronze horse
それぞれの門の前には青銅の馬が立っています
the horses neigh when the Bedouins come from the mountains
ベドウィンが山からやってくると馬が近づく
The walls of the city are cased with copper
街の壁は銅で覆われています
the watch-towers on the walls are roofed with brass
壁の望楼は真鍮で屋根が葺かれています
In every tower along the wall stands an archer
城壁沿いの塔には、弓兵が立っている
and each archer has a bow in his hand
そして、各射手は手に弓を持っています
At sunrise he strikes a gong with an arrow
日の出とともに銅鑼を矢で叩く
and at sunset he blows through a horn
そして夕暮れ時、彼は角笛を吹く
when I sought to enter the guards stopped me
私が入ろうとすると、警備員が私を止めました
and the guards asked of me who I was
そして、警備員は私が誰であるかを尋ねました
I made answer that I was a Dervish
私はダルヴィーシュだと答えました
I said I was on my way to the city of Mecca
私はメッカの街へ向かう途中だと言いました
in Mecca there was a green veil

メッカには緑のベールがありました
the Koran was embroidered with silver letters on it
コーランは銀色の文字で刺繍されていました
it was embroidered by the hands of the angels
天使の手によって刺繍されていました
the guards were filled with wonder at what I told them
警備員たちは、私が話したことに驚嘆していました
and they entreated me to enter the city
そして、彼らはわたしに町に入るように懇願した
Inside the city there was a bazaar
市内にはバザールがありました
Surely thou should'st have been with me
確かにあなたは私と一緒にいるべきだった
in the narrow streets the happy paper lanterns flutter
狭い路地には、幸せそうな提灯がはためく
they flutter like large butterflies
大きな蝶のように羽ばたく
When the wind blows they rise and fall like bubbles
風が吹くと泡のように上下します
In front of their booths sit the merchants
ブースの前には商人が座っています
every merchant sits on their silken carpets
すべての商人は絹の絨毯の上に座っています
They have long straight black beards
彼らは長くまっすぐな黒いあごひげを生やしています
and their turbans are covered with golden sequins
ターバンは金色のスパンコールで覆われています
they hold strings of amber and carved peach-stones
琥珀の紐と彫刻された桃の石が握られています
and they glide them through their cool fingers
そして、ひんやりとした指で滑らせます
Some of them sell galbanum and nard
ガルバナムやナードを売っているところもあります
some sell perfumes from the islands of the Indian Sea
インド洋の島々の香水を売るところもあります
and they sell the thick oil of red roses and myrrh
そして、赤いバラと没薬の濃厚な油を売っています

and they sell little nail-shaped cloves
そして、彼らは小さな釘の形をしたクローブを売っています
When one stops to speak to them they light frankincense
立ち止まって話しかけると、乳香を焚く
they throw pinches of it upon a charcoal brazier
彼らはそれを炭火鉢に投げつけます
and it makes the air sweet
そして、それは空気を甘くします
I saw a Syrian who held a thin rod
細い棒を持ったシリア人を見ました
grey threads of smoke came from the rod
棒から灰色の煙が上がっていた
and its odour was like the odour of the pink almonds
その匂いはピンクアーモンドの匂いのようでした
Others sell silver bracelets embossed with turquoise stones
また、ターコイズブルーの石をエンボス加工したシルバーの
ブレスレットを販売しているものもあります
and anklets of brass wire fringed with little pearls
そして、小さな真珠で縁取られた真鍮線のアンクレット
and tigers' claws set in gold
そして金にセットされた虎の爪
and the claws of that gilt cat
そして、あの金箔猫の爪
the the claws of leopards, also set in gold
ヒョウの爪も金でセットされています
and earrings of pierced emerald
エメラルドのピアス
and finger-rings of hollowed jade
そしてくり抜かれた翡翠の指輪
From the tea-houses came the sound of the guitar
茶室からギターの音が聞こえてきた
and the opium-smokers were in the tea-houses
そして、アヘンを吸う人たちは茶室にいた
their white smiling faces look out at the passers-by
白い笑顔が通行人を見つめる
thou truly should'st have been with me
汝は本当に私と共にいるべきだった

The wine-sellers elbow their way through the crowd
ワイン売りは群衆をかき分けて肘をつきます
with great black skins on their shoulders
肩に大きな黒い皮をかぶせて
Most of them sell the wine of Schiraz
それらのほとんどはスキラーズのワインを販売しています
the wine of Schiraz is as sweet as honey
スキラーズのワインは蜂蜜のように甘い
They serve it in little metal cups
彼らはそれを小さな金属製のカップで提供します
In the market-place stand the fruit sellers
市場では、果物売りが立っています
the fruit sellers sell all kinds of fruit
果物売りはあらゆる種類の果物を販売しています
ripe figs, with their bruised purple flesh
紫色の果肉が傷ついた熟したイチジク
melons, smelling of musk and yellow as topazes
メロン、トパーズのようにムスクと黄色の香りがする
citrons and rose-apples and clusters of white grapes
柚子とバラりんご、白ブドウの房
round red-gold oranges and oval lemons of green gold
ラウンドレッドゴールドオレンジとグリーンゴールドのオーバルレモン
Once I saw an elephant go by the fruit sellers
ある時、象が果物売りのそばを通り過ぎるのを見たことがあります
Its trunk was painted with vermilion and turmeric
その幹は朱色とターメリックで塗られていました
and over its ears it had a net of crimson silk cord
耳の上には真紅の絹の紐の網がついていました
It stopped opposite one of the booths
ブースの向かいに止まりました
and the elephant began eating the oranges
すると象はみかんを食べ始めました
instead of getting angry, the man only laughed
男は怒るどころか、ただ笑うだけだった
Thou canst not think how strange a people they are

汝は、彼らがどれほど奇妙な民族であるかを考えることができない
When they are glad they go to the bird-sellers
喜ぶと鳥売りのところへ行きます
they go to them to buy a caged bird
彼らは籠の鳥を買いに行きます
and they set the bird free to increase their joy
そして、彼らは鳥を自由にして、彼らの喜びを増します
and when they are sad they scourge themselves with thorns
悲しむと、いばらでむち打つ
so that their sorrow may not grow less
彼らの悲しみが減らないように

One evening I met some slaves
ある晩、私は何人かの奴隷に会った
they were carrying a heavy palanquin through the bazaar
彼らは重い輿を背負ってバザールを通り抜けていました
It was made of gilded bamboo
金箔を張った竹でできていました
and the poles were of vermilion lacquer
柱は朱色の漆でできていた
it was studded with brass peacocks
真鍮の孔雀がちりばめられていました
Across the windows hung thin curtains
窓の向こう側には薄いカーテンが掛けられていた
the curtains were embroidered with beetles' wings
カーテンにはカブトムシの羽が刺繍されていた
and they were lined with tiny seed-pearls
そして、小さな真珠の種が並んでいました
and as it passed by a pale-faced Circassian smiled at me
そして、それが通り過ぎるとき、青ざめた顔をしたチェルケス人が私に微笑みかけた
I followed behind bearers of the palanquin
私は駕籠の担ぎ手の後ろをついて行った
and the slaves hurried their steps and scowled
奴隷たちは急いで足を踏み出し、顔をしかめた
But I did not care if they scowled

しかし、彼らが顔をしかめても気にしなかった
I felt a great curiosity come over me
私は大きな好奇心が湧いてくるのを感じました
At last they stopped at a square white house
とうとう四角い白い家にたどり着きました
There were no windows to the house
家には窓がなかった
all the house had was a little door
家には小さなドアしかありませんでした
and the door was like the door of a tomb
その戸口は墓の扉のようだった
They set down the palanquin at the house
二人は輿を家に置いた
and they knocked three times with a copper hammer
そして、銅のハンマーで三度たたいた
An Armenian in a green leather caftan peered through the wicket
緑色の革のカフタンを着たアルメニア人が改札口から覗き込んでいた
and when he saw them he opened the door
そして、彼らを見ると、戸を開けた
he spread a carpet on the ground and the woman stepped out
彼が地面に絨毯を敷くと、女は出て行った
As she went in she turned round and smiled at me again
彼女が中に入ると、彼女は振り返って再び私に微笑みかけました
I had never seen anyone so pale
あんなに青白い人を見たのは初めてだった
When the moon rose I returned to the same place
月が昇ると、私は同じ場所に戻った
and I sought for the house, but it was no longer there
私はその家を探したが、それはもうなかった
When I saw that I knew who the woman was
それを見たとき、私はその女性が誰であるかを知った
and I knew why she had smiled at me
そして、なぜ彼女が私に微笑んだのかがわかった

Certainly, thou should'st have been with me
確かに、あなたは私と一緒にいるべきでした

There was a feast of the New Moon
新月の饗宴があった
the young Emperor came forth from his palace
若い皇帝が宮殿から出てきた
and he went into the mosque to pray
そして、礼拝のためにモスクに入った
His hair and beard were dyed with rose-leaves
髪と髭は薔薇の葉で染められていた
and his cheeks were powdered with a fine gold dust
頬には細かい金粉がまぶされていた
The palms of his feet and hands were yellow with saffron
彼の足と手のひらはサフランで黄色くなっていました
At sunrise he went forth from his palace
日の出とともに、王子は宮殿から出て行きました
he was dressed in a robe of silver
彼は銀のローブを着ていた
and at sunset he returned again
そして日が暮れると、また戻って来ました
then he was dressed in a robe of gold
それから彼は金の衣をまといました
The people flung themselves on the ground
人々は地面に身を投げた
they hid their faces, but I would not do so
彼らは顔を隠したが、私はそうはしなかった
I stood by the stall of a seller of dates and waited
私はデーツ売りの屋台のそばに立って待ちました
When the Emperor saw me he raised his painted eyebrows
皇帝陛下は私を見ると、眉をひそめた
and he stopped to observe me
そして彼は立ち止まって私を観察した
I stood quite still and made him no obeisance
私はじっと立っていて、彼に服従させなかった
The people marvelled at my boldness
人々は私の大胆さに驚嘆しました

they counselled me to flee from the city
彼らは私に街から逃げるように勧めました
but I paid no heed to their warnings
しかし、私は彼らの警告に耳を傾けませんでした
instead, I went and sat with the sellers of strange gods
その代わりに、私は奇妙な神々の売り子たちのところに行って座りました
by reason of their craft they are abominated
その技術ゆえに、彼らは忌み嫌われている
When I told them what I had done each of them gave me an idol
私がしたことを彼らに話すと、彼らはそれぞれ私に偶像を与えました
and they prayed me to leave them
そして、彼らはわたしに彼らから離れるようにと祈った

That night I was in the Street of Pomegranates
その夜、私はザクロの街にいました
I was in a tea-house and I laid on a cushion
私は喫茶店にいて、座布団の上に横たわっていました
the guards of the Emperor entered and led me to the palace
皇帝の護衛が入ってきて、私を宮殿に連れて行ってくれました
As I went in they closed each door behind me
私が中に入ると、彼らは私の後ろでドアを閉めました
and they put a chain across each door
そして、彼らはそれぞれのドアに鎖を掛けました
Inside the palace there was a great courtyard
宮殿の中には大きな中庭がありました
The walls of the courtyard were of white alabaster
中庭の壁は白いアラバスターでできていた
the alabaster was decorated with blue and green tiles
アラバスターは青と緑のタイルで飾られていました
and the pillars were of green marble
柱は緑の大理石でできていた
and the pavement was of peach-blossom marble
舗道は桃の花の大理石でできていた

I had never seen anything like it before
こんなの見たことないよ
As I passed the courtyard two veiled women were on a balcony
中庭を通り過ぎると、ベールをかぶった二人の女性がバルコニーにいた
they looked down from their balcony and cursed me
彼らはベランダから見下ろし、私を罵った
The guards hastened on through the courtyard
衛兵たちは中庭を急いで進んだ
the butts of the lances rang upon the polished floor
槍の尻が磨かれた床に響いた
They opened a gate of wrought ivory
彼らは錬金された象牙の門を開いた
I found myself in a watered garden of seven terraces
気がつくと、そこは7つのテラスからなる水やりの庭だった
The garden was planted with tulip-cups and moon-flowers
庭にはチューリップカップと月花が植えられていました
a fountain hung in the dusky air like a slim reed of crystal
薄暗い空気に浮かぶ噴水は、水晶の細い葦のようだった
The cypress-trees were like burnt-out torches
糸杉の木は燃え尽きた松明のようだった
From one of the trees a nightingale was singing
一本の木からナイチンゲールが歌っていた
At the end of the garden stood a little pavilion
庭の端には小さなパビリオンが立っていました
while we approached the pavilion two eunuchs came out
パビリオンに近づくと、2人の宦官が出てきました
Their fat bodies swayed as they walked
太った体が歩くたびに揺れていた
and they glanced curiously at me
そして、彼らは不思議そうに私を一瞥しました
One of them drew aside the captain of the guard
そのうちの一人が衛兵隊長を脇に引き寄せた
and in a low voice the eunuch whispered to him
そして低い声で宦官が彼にささやいた
The other kept munching scented pastilles

もう一人は香りのするトローチをむしゃむしゃ食べ続けた
these he took out of an oval box of lilac enamel
彼は薄紫色のエナメルの楕円形の箱から取り出した
soon after the captain of the guard dismissed the soldiers
間もなく、衛兵隊長が兵士たちを解散させた
The soldiers went back to the palace
兵士たちは宮殿に戻りました
the eunuchs followed behind the guards, but slowly
宦官たちは衛兵の後ろを追ったが、ゆっくりとした
and they plucked the sweet mulberries from the trees
そして、木から甘い桑の実を摘み取りました
at one time the older eunuch turned round
ある時、年配の宦官が振り向いた
and he smiled at me with an evil smile
そして、彼は邪悪な笑みを浮かべて私に微笑みかけた
Then the captain of the guards motioned me forwards
その時、衛兵隊長が私を前に進めた
I walked to the entrance without trembling
震えもせずに玄関まで歩いていきました
I drew the heavy curtain aside, and entered
私は重いカーテンを脇に引いて中に入った
The young Emperor was stretched on a couch
若き皇帝は長椅子に横たわっていた
the couch was covered in dyed lion skins
ソファは染めたライオンの皮で覆われていた
and a falcon was perched upon his wrist
そして、鷹が彼の手首にとまっていた
Behind him stood a brass-turbaned Nubian
彼の背後には、真鍮のターバンを巻いたヌビア人が立っていた
he was naked down to the waist
腰まで裸だった
he had heavy earrings in his split ears
彼は割れた耳に重いイヤリングをしていた
On a table by the side lay a mighty scimitar of steel
脇のテーブルの上には、巨大な鋼鉄のシミターが置かれていた

When the Emperor saw me he frowned
皇帝は私を見ると眉をひそめた
he asked me, "What is thy name?"
彼は私に尋ねた、「あなたの名前は何ですか?」
"Knowest thou not that I am Emperor of this city?"
「汝は、私がこの都市の皇帝であることを知らないのか?」
But I made him no answer to his question
しかし、私は彼の質問に何の答えもしなかった
He pointed with his finger at the scimitar
彼は指でシミターを指差した
the Nubian seized the scimitar, ready to fight
ヌビア人はシミターを掴み、戦う準備をした
rushing forward he struck at me with great violence
突進してきて、彼は猛烈な勢いで私を殴りつけた
The blade whizzed through me and did me no hurt
刃は私を貫いたが、私には傷つけられなかった
The man fell sprawling on the floor
男は床に崩れ落ちた
when he rose up his teeth chattered with terror
彼が立ち上がると、恐怖で歯がガタガタと音を立てた
and he hid behind the couch
そして彼はソファの後ろに隠れました
The Emperor leapt to his feet
皇帝は跳び上がった
he took a lance from a stand and threw it at me
彼はスタンドから槍を取り出し、私に投げつけた
I caught it in its flight
私はその飛行でそれを捕まえました
I broke the shaft into two pieces
シャフトを2つに折ってみました
then he shot at me with an arrow
それから彼は矢で私を撃った
but I held up my hands as it came to me
しかし、私はそれが来ると手をかざしました
and I stopped the arrow in mid-air
そして私は空中で矢を止めた
Then he drew a dagger from a belt of white leather

そして白い革のベルトから短剣を抜いた
and he stabbed the Nubian in the throat
そしてヌビア人の喉を刺した
so that the the slave would not tell of his dishonour
奴隷が自分の不名誉を言わないように
The man writhed like a trampled snake
男は踏みつけられた蛇のように身悶えした
and a red foam bubbled from his lips
そして、唇から赤い泡が泡立った
As soon as he was dead the Emperor turned to me
彼が死ぬとすぐに、皇帝は私の方を向いた
he took out a little napkin of purple silk
彼は紫色の絹の小さなナプキンを取り出した
and he had wiped away the bright sweat from his brow
そして額の汗をぬぐった
he said to me, "Art thou a prophet?"
彼は私に言った、「あなたは預言者ですか」。
"is it that I may not harm thee?"
「わたしがあなたを傷つけないようにするためか」。
"or are you the son of a prophet?"
「それとも預言者の息子か?」
"and is it that can I do thee no hurt?"
「それで、お前を傷つけないでいられるのか?」
"I pray thee leave my city tonight"
「今夜、汝が私の町を去ることを祈る」
"while thou art in my city I am no longer its lord"
「あなたが私の町にいる間、私はもはやその主ではありません」
And this time I answered his question
そして今回、私は彼の質問に答えました
"I will leave they city, for half of thy treasure"
「わたしは彼らの町を去ります。あなたの財宝の半分のために」
"Give me half of thy treasure and I will go away"
「あなたの宝物の半分をください。そうすれば、私は立ち去ります」
"He took me by the hand and led me into the garden"

「彼は私の手を取って、庭に連れて行きました」
"When the captain of the guard saw me he wondered"
「衛兵隊長は私を見て不思議に思った」
"When the eunuchs saw me their knees shook"
「宦官たちは私を見て膝を震わせた」
"and they fell upon the ground in fear"
「彼らは恐れて地にひれ伏した」

There is a special chamber in the palace
宮殿には特別な部屋があります
the chamber has eight walls of red porphyry
部屋には8つの赤い斑岩の壁があります
and it has a brass-scaled ceiling hung with lamps
真鍮製の天井にはランプが吊るされています
The Emperor touched one of the walls and it opened
皇帝が壁の1つに触れると、壁が開きました
we passed down a corridor that was lit with many torches
たくさんの松明で照らされた廊下を通り過ぎました
In niches upon each side stood great wine-jars
両側のくぼみには、大きなワインの壺が立っていました
the wine-jars were filled to the brim with silver pieces
葡萄酒の壺は銀のかけらでいっぱいでした
soon we reached the centre of the corridor
やがて廊下の真ん中に着いた
the Emperor spoke the word that may not be spoken
皇帝は語られてはならない言葉を語られた
a granite door swung back on a secret spring
花崗岩の扉が秘密の泉に揺れた
and he put his hands before his face
そして両手を顔の前に置いた
so that he would not be dazzled
目がくらまないように
Thou would not have believed how marvellous a place it was
汝は、それがどんなに素晴らしい場所であるかを信じなかっただろう
There were huge tortoise-shells full of pearls

真珠でいっぱいの巨大な亀の甲羅がありました
and there were hollowed moonstones of great size
そして、大きな大きさのくり抜かれたムーンストーンがありました
the moonstones were piled up with red rubies
ムーンストーンには赤いルビーが積み上げられていました
The gold was stored in coffers of elephant-hide
金塊は象の皮の金庫に保管されていた
and there was gold-dust in leather bottles
そして、革瓶に入った砂金がありました
There were more opals and sapphires than I could count
数えきれないほどのオパールとサファイアがありました
the many opals were kept in cups of crystal
多くのオパールはクリスタルのカップに保管されていました
and the sapphires were kept in cups of jade
そして、サファイアは翡翠のカップに保管されていました
Round green emeralds were arranged in order
丸いグリーンエメラルドが順番に並べられていました
they were laid out upon thin plates of ivory
それらは象牙の薄い板の上に並べられていた
in one corner were silk bags full of turquoise-stones
片隅には、ターコイズブルーの石でいっぱいの絹の袋がありました
and others bags were filled with beryls
他の袋は緑柱石でいっぱいでした
The ivory horns were heaped with purple amethysts
象牙の角には紫色のアメジストが山盛りに
and the horns of brass were heaped with chalcedony and sard stones
真鍮の角にはカルセドニーとサードの石が積み上げられていた
The pillars holding the ceiling were made of cedar
天井を支える柱は杉でできていました
they were hung with strings of yellow lynx-stones
黄色いオオヤマネコの石の紐で吊るされていた
In the flat oval shields there were carbuncles
平らな楕円形の盾にはカーバンクルがありました

they were wine-coloured, and coloured like grass
それらは葡萄色で、草のような色をしていた
And yet I have told thee but a fraction of what was there
それなのに、わたしはそこにあったことのほんの一部しかあなたに話さなかった

The Emperor took away his hands from his face
皇帝は両手を顔から離した
he said to me, "this is my house of treasure"
彼は私に「ここは私の宝の家だ」と言いました
half of what is in this house is thine
この家にあるものの半分はあなたのものです
this is as I promised to thee
これはわたしがあなたに約束したとおりである
And I will give thee camels and camel drivers
わたしはあなたにらくだとらくだの御者を与えよう
and the camel drivers shall do thy bidding
らくだの御者は、あなたの言いつけを行なうであろう
please, take thy share of the treasure
どうか、その財宝の分け前を受け取ってください
take it to whatever part of the world thou desirest
汝が望む世界のどこへでも持って行け
But the thing shall be done tonight
しかし、事は今夜成し遂げられるであろう
because, as you know, the sun is my father
なぜなら、ご存じの通り、太陽は私の父だからです
he must not see a man in the city that I cannot slay
彼は、わたしが殺すことのできない者を、この町で見てはならない
But I answered him, "The gold that is here is thine"
しかし、私は彼に答えました、「ここにある金はあなたのものです」
"and the silver that is here also is thine"
「そして、ここにある銀もまた、あなたのものです」
"and thine are the precious jewels and opals"
「そして、あなたは貴重な宝石とオパールです」
"As for me, I have no need of these treasures"

「私には、これらの宝物は必要ない」
"I shall not take anything from thee"
「わたしはあなたから何も奪わない」
"but I will take the little ring that thou wearest"
「しかし、私はあなたが着けている小さな指輪を取ります」
"it is on the finger of thy hand"
「それはあなたの手の指の上にあります」
when I said this the Emperor frowned
私がそう言うと、皇帝は眉をひそめた
"It is but a ring of lead," he cried
「あれは鉛の輪にすぎない」と彼は叫んだ
"a simple ring has no value for you"
「シンプルな指輪はあなたにとって価値がない」
"take thy half of the treasure and go from my city"
「宝の半分を取って、わたしの町から出て行け」
"Nay" I answered, "it is what I want"
「いや」と私は答えた、「それは私が望むものです」
"I will take nought but that lead ring"
「あのリードリング以外は何も取らない」
"for I know what is written within it"
「わたしは、その中に何が書いてあるかを知っているからである」
"and I know for what purpose it is"
「そして、私はそれが何のためにあるのか知っています」
And the Emperor trembled in fear
皇帝は恐怖に震え上がった
he besought me and said, "Take all the treasure"
彼はわたしに懇願し、「すべての宝物を取りなさい」と言いました
"take all the treasure and go from my city"
「すべての宝物を持って、私の町から去って行きなさい」
"The half that is mine shall be thine also"
「わたしの半分もあなたのものになる」

And I did a strange thing
そして、私は奇妙なことをしました
but what I did matters not

しかし、私が何をしたかは重要ではありません
because there is a cave that is but a day's journey from here
なぜなら、ここから1日しかかからない洞窟があるからです
in that cave I have hidden the Ring of Riches
あの洞窟に、私は富の指輪を隠した
in this cave the ring of riches waits for thy coming
この洞窟では、富の輪があなたの到来を待っています
He who has this Ring is richer than all the kings of the world
この指輪を持つ者は、この世のすべての王よりも裕福である
Come and take it, and the world's riches shall be thine
来てそれを取りなさい、そうすれば世界の富は汝のものになるであろう
But the young Fisherman laughed, "love is better than riches"
しかし、若い漁師は「愛は富にまさる」と笑いました
"and the little Mermaid loves me," he added
「そして、人魚姫は私を愛しています」と彼は付け加えました
"Nay, but there is nothing better than riches," said the Soul
「いや、でも富に勝るものはない」と魂は言いました
"Love is better," answered the young Fisherman
「愛のほうがいいよ」と若い漁師は答えました
and he plunged back into the deep waters
そして、彼は深海に飛び込みました
and the Soul went weeping away over the marshes
そして、魂は沼地の上で泣きながら去って行きました

After the Third Year
3年目以降

it had been three year since he cast his soul away
彼が魂を捨ててから3年が経っていた
the Soul came back to the shore of the sea
魂は海の岸に帰ってきた
and the Soul called to the young Fisherman
そして魂は若い漁師に呼ばれました
the young Fisherman rose back out of the sea
若い漁師は海から上がりました
he asked his soul, "Why dost thou call me?"
彼は魂に尋ねた、「なぜ私を呼んだのですか」。
And the Soul answered, "Come nearer"
すると魂は「もっと近づいてきなさい」と答えた
"come nearer, so that I may speak with thee"
「わたしがあなたと話すために、もっと近づいてきなさい」
"I have seen marvellous things"
「私は素晴らしいものを見てきました」
So the young Fisherman came nearer to his soul
それで、若い漁師は彼の魂に近づきました
and he couched in the shallow water
そして彼は浅瀬に身を潜めた
and he leaned his head upon his hand
そして、その手に頭をもたせかけた
and he listened to his Soul
そして彼は自分の魂に耳を傾けた
and his Soul spoke to him
そして彼の魂は彼に語りかけた

In a city that I know of there is an inn
私の知っている街に宿屋がある
the inn that I speak of stands by a river
私が話す宿は川のほとりに建っています
in this inn I sat and drunk with sailors
この宿屋で、私は船乗りたちと座って酒を飲んだ
sailors who drank two different coloured wines

2種類のワインを飲んだ船乗りたち
and they ate bread made of barley
そして、大麦で作ったパンを食べた
and I ate salty little fish with them
そして、私は彼らと一緒に塩辛い小さな魚を食べました
little fish that were served in bay leaves with vinegar
酢で月桂樹の葉に添えられた小さな魚
while we sat and made merry an old man entered
私たちが座って陽気にしている間に、一人の老人が入ってきました
he had a leather carpet with him
彼は革の絨毯を持っていた
and he had a lute that had two horns of amber
そして、琥珀の角が二本あるリュートを持っていた
he laid out the carpet on the floor
彼は床に絨毯を敷いた
and he struck on the strings of his lute
そして彼はリュートの弦を叩いた
and a girl ran in and began to dance in front of us
すると女の子が走ってきて、私たちの前で踊り始めました
Her face was veiled with a veil of gauze
彼女の顔はガーゼのベールで覆われていた
and she was wearing silk, but her feet were naked
絹の服を着ていたが、足は裸だった
and her feet moved over the carpet like little white pigeons
そして、彼女の足は小さな白い鳩のように絨毯の上を動きました
Never have I seen anything so marvellous
こんなに素晴らしいものは見たことがない
the city where she dances is but a day's journey from here
彼女が踊る街は、ここから1日の旅に過ぎない
the young Fisherman heard the words of his Soul
若い漁師は彼の魂の言葉を聞いた
he remembered that the little Mermaid had no feet
彼は人魚姫に足がなかったことを思い出しました
and he remembered she was unable to dance
そして、彼は彼女が踊ることができなかったことを思い出し

ました
a great desire came over him to see the girl
少女に会いたいという大きな欲求が彼に襲い掛かってきた
he said to himself, "It is but a day's journey"
彼は自分に言い聞かせた、「それは一日の旅に過ぎない」
"and then I can return to my love," he laughed
「そうすれば、僕は愛する元に戻れるんだ」と彼は笑った
he stood up in the shallow water
彼は浅瀬で立ち上がった
and he strode towards the shore
そして、大股で岸の方へ向かった
when he had reached the dry shore he laughed again
乾いた岸に着くと、また笑いました
and he held out his arms to his Soul
そして、両腕を自分の魂に差し出した
his Soul gave a great cry of joy
彼の魂は大きな喜びの叫びをあげた
his Soul ran to meet his body
彼の魂は彼の体に会うために走った
and his Soul entered into back him again
そして、彼の魂は再び彼の背後に入っていった
the young Fisherman became one with his shadow once more
若い漁師は再び自分の影と一つになりました
the shadow of the body that is the body of the Soul
魂の体である体の影
And his Soul said to him, "Let us not tarry"
彼の魂は彼に言った、「とどまらないでください」。
"but let us get going at once"
「でも、さっさと始めよう」
"because the Sea-gods are jealous"
「海の神々が嫉妬しているから」
"and they have monsters that do their bidding"
「そして、彼らには彼らの命令に従うモンスターがいます」
So they made haste to get to the city
それで、彼らは急いで町に着きました

Sin
罪

all that night they journeyed beneath the moon
その夜、二人は月の下を旅した
and all the next day they journeyed beneath the sun
そして次の日、二人は太陽の下を旅した
on the evening of the day they came to a city
その日の夕方、彼らはある町に来ました
the young Fisherman asked his Soul
若い漁師は彼の魂に尋ねました
"Is this the city in which she dances?"
「ここは彼女が踊る街なの？」
And his Soul answered him
そして彼の魂は彼に答えた
"It is not this city, but another"
「この街ではなく、別の街だ」
"Nevertheless, let us enter this city"
「それでも、この街に入ろう」
So they entered the city and passed through the streets
それで、彼らは町に入り、通りを通り抜けました
they passed through the street of jewellers
彼らは宝石商の通りを通り抜けました
passing through the street, the young Fisherman saw a silver cup
通りを通り過ぎると、若い漁師は銀のカップを見つけました
his Soul said to him, "Take that silver cup"
彼の魂は彼に言った、「その銀の杯を取りなさい」
and his Soul told him to hide the silver cup
そして彼の魂は彼に銀の杯を隠すように言いました
So he took the silver cup and hid it
それで、彼は銀の杯を取って隠しました
and they went hurriedly out of the city
そして、彼らは急いで町を出て行きました
the young Fisherman frowned and flung the cup away
若い漁師は眉をひそめ、カップを投げ捨てました
"Why did'st thou tell me to take this cup?"

「なぜ、この杯を飲めと言わなかったのですか?」
"it was an evil thing to do"
「それは邪悪なことだった」
But his Soul just told him to be at peace
しかし、彼の魂はただ彼に安らぎなさいと言いました

on the evening of the second day they came to a city
二日目の夕方、二人はある町に着いた
the young Fisherman asked his Soul
若い漁師は彼の魂に尋ねました
"Is this the city in which she dances?"
「ここは彼女が踊る街なの?」
And his Soul answered him
そして彼の魂は彼に答えた
"It is not this city, but another"
「この街ではなく、別の街だ」
"Nevertheless, let us enter this city"
「それでも、この街に入ろう」
So they entered in and passed through the streets
それで、彼らは中に入って通りを通り抜けた
they passed through the street of sandal sellers
二人はサンダル売りの通りを通り過ぎた
passing through the street, the young Fisherman saw a child
通りを通り過ぎると、若い漁師は子供を見ました
the child was standing by a jar of water
子供は水の入った瓶のそばに立っていました
his Soul told him to smite the child
彼の魂は彼に子供を打つように言いました
So he smote the child till it wept
それで、子供が泣くまで打った
after he had done this they went hurriedly out of the city
イエスがこれを済ませると、かれらは急いで町を出て行った
the young Fisherman grew angry with his soul
若い漁師は自分の魂に怒りを覚えました
"Why did'st thou tell me to smite the child?"
「なぜ、あの子を打てと言わなかったのですか?」
"it was an evil thing to do"

「それは邪悪なことだった」
But his Soul just told him to be at peace
しかし、彼の魂はただ彼に安らぎなさいと言いました

And on the evening of the third day they came to a city
そして三日目の夕方、彼らはある町に着いた
the young Fisherman asked his Soul
若い漁師は彼の魂に尋ねました
"Is this the city in which she dances?"
「ここは彼女が踊る街なの?」
And his Soul answered him
そして彼の魂は彼に答えた
"It may be that it is this city, so let us enter"
「もしかしたら、この街かもしれないから、入ろう」
So they entered the city and passed through the streets
それで、彼らは町に入り、通りを通り抜けました
but nowhere could the young Fisherman find the river
しかし、若い漁師はどこにも川を見つけることができませんでした
and he couldn't find the inn either
そして、宿も見つからなかった
And the people of the city looked curiously at him
町の人々は不思議そうに彼を見つめました
and he grew afraid and asked his Soul to leave
そして彼は恐れを募らせ、自分の魂に立ち去るように頼みました
"she who dances with white feet is not here"
「白い足で踊る女はここにはいない」
But his Soul answered "Nay, but let us rest"
しかし、彼の魂は「いや、休もう」と答えました
"because the night is dark"
「夜が暗いから」
"and there will be robbers on the way"
「そして、途中で強盗がいるでしょう」
So he sat himself down in the market-place and rested
それで、彼は市場に座って休んだ
after a time a hooded merchant walked past him

しばらくすると、フードをかぶった商人が彼の前を通り過ぎた
he had a cloak of cloth of Tartary
彼はタルタリアの布の外套を羽織っていた
and he carried a lantern of pierced horn
そして、角笛の刺し籠を持っていた
the merchant asked the young Fisherman
商人は若い漁師に尋ねました
"Why dost thou sit in the market-place?"
「なぜ市場に座っているのですか?」
"the booths are closed and the bales corded"
「ブースは閉鎖され、ベールはコードで結ばれています」
And the young Fisherman answered him
すると、若い漁師は彼に答えました
"I can find no inn in this city"
「この街には宿屋がない」
"I have no kinsman who might give me shelter"
「私には、私をかくまってくれる親族がいない」
"Are we not all kinsmen?" said the merchant
「みんな親戚じゃないの?」と商人は言いました
"And did not one God make us?"
そして、唯一の神が私たちを造られたのではありませんか?
"come with me, for I have a guest-chamber"
「いっしょに来い。客間があるから」
So the young Fisherman rose up and followed the merchant
それで若い漁師は立ち上がり、商人の後を追った
they passed through a garden of pomegranates
彼らはザクロの庭を通り抜けました
and they entered into the house of the merchant
そして、商人の家に入った
the merchant brought him rose-water in a copper dish
商人は銅の皿に入った薔薇の水を持ってきました
so that he could wash his hands
手を洗うために
and he brought him ripe melons
そして熟したメロンを持ってきてくれた
so that he could quench his thirst

喉の渇きを癒すために
and he gave him a bowl of rice
そして、ご飯の入った茶碗をくれました
in the bowl of rice was roasted lamb
ご飯のボウルには子羊のローストがありました
so that he could satisfy his hunger
飢えを満たせるように
the young Fischerman finished his meal
若いフィッシャーマンは食事を終えた
and he thanked the merchant for all his generousity
そして、商人の寛大さに感謝しました
then the merchant led him to the guest-chamber
それから商人は彼を客間に連れて行きました
and the merchant let him sleep in his chamber
商人は彼を自分の部屋で眠らせました
the young Fisherman gave him thanks again
若い漁師は彼にもう一度感謝しました
and he kissed the ring that was on his hand
そして、手にはめていた指輪にキスをした
he flung himself down on the carpets of dyed goat's-hair
彼は染めた山羊の毛の絨毯の上に身を投げ出した
And when pulled the blanket over himself he fell asleep
そして、毛布をかぶせると、眠りに落ちました

it was three hours before dawn
夜明けの3時間前だった
while it was still night his Soul woke him
まだ夜なのに、彼の魂は彼を目覚めさせた
his Soul told him to rise
彼の魂は彼に立ち上がるように言いました
"Rise up and go to the room of the merchant"
「起きて商人の部屋へ行け」
"go to the room in which he sleeps"
「彼が寝ている部屋に行きなさい」
"slay him in his sleep"
「眠っている間に殺せ」
"take his gold from him"

「彼から彼の金を奪え」
"because we have need of it"
「必要だから」
And the young Fisherman rose up
そして若い漁師は立ち上がった
and he crept towards the room of the merchant
そして、商人の部屋に忍び寄りました
there was a curved sword at the feet of the merchant
商人の足元には湾曲した剣があった
and there was a tray by the side of the merchant
そして、商人のそばに盆がありました
the tray held nine purses of gold
トレイには金の入った財布が9つ入っていました
And he reached out his hand and touched the sword
そして手を伸ばして剣に触れた
and when he touched the sword the merchant woke up
そして、剣に触れると、商人は目を覚ましました
he leapt up and seized the sword
彼は跳び上がり、剣を掴んだ
"Dost thou return evil for good?"
「汝は悪を善として返すのか?」
"do you pay with the shedding of blood?"
「血を流すことで償うのか?」
"in return for the kindness that I have shown thee"
「わたしがあなたに示した親切のお返しに」
And his Soul said to the young Fisherman, "Strike him"
そして、彼の魂は若い漁師に言った、「彼を打て」
and he struck him so that he swooned
そして、彼は気絶したので、彼を打った
he seized the nine purses of gold
彼は9つの金の財布をつかんだ
and he fled hastily through the garden of pomegranates
そして、ザクロの園を急いで逃げました
and he set his face to the star of morning
そして彼は朝の星に顔を向けた
they escaped the city without being noticed
彼らは気づかれることなく街を脱出した

the young Fisherman beat his breast
若い漁師は胸を叩いた
"Why didst thou bid me to slay the merchant?"
「なぜ私に商人を殺すよう命じたのですか?」
"why did you make me take his gold?"
「どうして金を奪わせたの?」
"Surely thou art evil"
「汝は確かに邪悪だ」
But his Soul told him to be at peace
しかし、彼の魂は彼に安らぎを告げました
"No!" cried the young Fisherman
「だめだ!」と若い漁師は叫びました
"I can not be at peace with this"
「これでは平穏になれない」
"all that thou hast made me do I hate"
「あなたがわたしにさせたすべてのことは、わたしを憎む」
"and what else I hate is you"
「他に嫌いなのはお前だ」
"why have you brought me here to do these things?"
「どうして私をここに連れてきて、こんなことをしたの?」
And his Soul answered him
そして彼の魂は彼に答えた
"When you sent me into the world you gave me no heart"
「あなたが私をこの世に送ったとき、あなたは私に心を与えませんでした」
"so I learned to do all these things"
だから、私はこれらすべてのことをすることを学びました
"and I learned to love these things"
「そして、私はこれらのものを愛することを学びました」
"What sayest thou?" murmured the young Fisherman
「おまえは何を言っているんだ?」と若い漁師はつぶやきました
"Thou knowest," answered his Soul
「汝は知っている」と彼の魂は答えた
"Have you forgotten that you gave me no heart?"
「お前は俺に心臓を与えなかったことを忘れたのか?」
"don't trouble yourself for me, but be at peace"

「私のために悩まないで、安らかに」
"because there is no pain you shouldn't give away"
「与えてはいけない痛みがないから」
"and there is no pleasure that you should not receive"
「そして、あなたが受けてはならない喜びはありません」
when the young Fisherman heard these words he trembled
若い漁師はこの言葉を聞いて震え上がりました
"Nay, but thou art evil"
「いや、だがお前は邪悪だ」
"you have made me forget my love"
「あなたは私に私の愛を忘れさせました」
"you have tempted me with temptations"
「あなたは誘惑で私を誘惑しました」
"and you have set my feet in the ways of sin"
「あなたはわたしを罪の道に立たせた」
And his Soul answered him
そして彼の魂は彼に答えた
"you have not forgotten?"
「忘れてないの?」
"you sent me into the world with no heart"
「あなたは私を心のない世界に送りました」
"Come, let us go to another city"
「さあ、別の街に行こう」
"let us make merry with the gold we have"
「今ある金でお祭り騒ぎをしよう」
But the young Fisherman took the nine purses of gold
しかし、若い漁師は金の入った財布を9つ持っていきました
he flung the purses of gold into the sand
彼は金の入った財布を砂に投げ捨てた
and he trampled on the on the purses of gold
そして、金の財布を踏みにじった
"Nay!" he cried to his Soul
「いやだ!」彼は魂に向かって叫んだ
"I will have nought to do with thee"
「私はあなたとは何の関係もありません」
"I will not journey with thee anywhere"
「私はあなたと一緒にどこにも旅をしません」

"I have sent thee away before"
「わたしは前にあなたを追い払った」
"and I will send thee away again"
「わたしはまたあなたを追い払う」
"because thou hast brought me no good"
「あなたがわたしに何の役にも立たなかったからだ」
And he turned his back to the moon
そして彼は月に背を向けた
he held the little green knife in his hand
彼は小さな緑色のナイフを手に持っていた
he strove to cut from his feet the shadow of the body
彼は足元から死体の影を切ろうと努めた
the shadow of the body, which is the body of the Soul
魂の体である体の影
Yet his Soul stirred not from him
しかし、彼の魂は彼から動揺しませんでした
and it paid no heed to his command
そして、それは彼の命令に注意を払わなかった
"The spell the Witch told thee avails no more"
「魔女がお前に言った呪文はもう役に立たない」
"I may not leave thee anymore"
「もうお前から離れられないかもしれない」
"and thou can't drive me forth"
「そして、あなたは私を追い出すことはできません」
"Once in his life may a man send his Soul away"
「人生で一度、人が自分の魂を送り出すことができますように」
"but he who receives back his Soul must keep it for ever"
「しかし、自分の魂を取り戻す者は、それを永遠に保たなければならない」
"this is his punishment and his reward"
「これが彼の罰であり、彼の報酬である」
the young Fisherman grew pale at his fate
若い漁師は自分の運命に青ざめました
and he clenched his hands and cried
そして両手を握りしめて泣いた
"She was a false Witch for not telling me"

「あの子は私に言わなかった偽りの魔女だった」
"Nay," answered his Soul, "she was not a false Witch"
「いや、」と彼の魂は答えた、「彼女は偽りの魔女ではなかった」
"but she was true to Him she worships"
「しかし、彼女は彼女が崇拝する彼に忠実でした」
"and she will be his servant forever"
「そして、彼女は永遠に彼のしもべとなるでしょう」
the young Fisherman knew he could not get rid of his Soul again
若い漁師は、自分の魂を二度と取り除くことはできないことを知っていました
he knew now that his soul was an evil Soul
彼は今や、自分の魂が邪悪な魂であることを知った
and his Soul would abide with him always
そうすれば、彼の魂はいつも彼と共にある
when he knew this he fell upon the ground and wept
これを知ると、彼は地面にひれ伏して泣きました

- 83 -

The Heart
心臓

when it was day the young Fisherman rose up
昼間、若い漁師は立ち上がった
he told his Soul, "I will bind my hands"
彼は自分の魂に「私は私の手を縛る」と言いました
"that way I can not do thy bidding"
「そうすれば、私はあなたの命令に従うことはできません」
"and I will close my lips"
「唇を閉ざす」
"that way I can not speak thy words"
「そうすれば、私はあなたの言葉を話すことができません」
"and I will return to the place where my love lives"
「そして、私は私の愛する場所に戻ります」
"to the sea will I return"
「海に帰る」
"I will return to where she sung to me"
「彼女が歌ってくれた場所へ帰る」
"and I will call to her"
「わたしは彼女を呼ぶ」
"I will tell her the evil I have done"
「私がした悪事を彼女に話してやる」
"and I will tell her the evil thou hast wrought on me"
「そして、あなたがわたしに下した災いを彼女に告げよう」
his Soul tempted him, "Who is thy love?"
彼の魂は彼を誘惑した、「あなたの愛は誰ですか」。
"why should thou return to her?"
「なぜ彼女のところに戻らなければならないのですか?」
"The world has many fairer than she is"
「世界には彼女よりも公平な人がたくさんいる」
"There are the dancing-girls of Samaris"
「サマリスの踊り子がいる」
"they dance the way birds dance"
「鳥が踊るように踊る」
"and they dance the way beasts dance"
「そして彼らは獣が踊るように踊る」

"Their feet are painted with henna"
「彼らの足はヘナで塗られている」
"in their hands they have little copper bells"
「彼らの手には小さな銅の鐘がある」
"They laugh while they dance"
「踊りながら笑う」
"their laughter is as clear as the laughter of water"
「彼らの笑い声は水の笑い声のように澄んでいる」
"Come with me and I will show them to thee"
わたしと一緒に来なさい。わたしが彼らに見せてあげよう
"because why trouble yourself with things of sin?"
「だって、なぜ罪のことで悩むのか？」
"Is that which is pleasant to eat not made to be eaten?"
「食べて楽しいものは、食べるために作られているのではないのか？」
"Is there poison in that which is sweet to drink?"
「飲むのに甘いものには毒があるのか？」
"Trouble not thyself, but come with me to another city"
「わざわざ悩むな。わたしと一緒に他の町に来なさい」
"There is a little city with a garden of tulip-trees"
「ユリノキの庭がある小さな街がある」
"in its garden there are white peacocks"
「庭には白い孔雀がいる」
"and there are peacocks that have blue breasts"
「そして、青い胸を持つ孔雀がいます」
"Their tails are like disks of ivory"
「尻尾は象牙の円盤のようだ」
"when they spread their tails in the sun"
「太陽の下で尻尾を広げるとき」
"And she who feeds them dances for their pleasure"
「そして、彼らを養う女は、彼らの快楽のために踊る」
"and sometimes she dances on her hands"
「そして時々、彼女は彼女の手の上で踊る」
"and at other times she dances with her feet"
「そしてまたある時は、彼女は自分の足で踊る」
"Her eyes are coloured with stibium"
「彼女の目はスティビウムで着色されている」

"her nostrils are shaped like the wings of a swallow"
「鼻の穴はツバメの羽のような形をしている」
"and she laughs while she dances"
「そして彼女は踊りながら笑う」
"and the silver rings on her ankles ring"
「そして、彼女の足首の銀の指輪」
"Don't trouble thyself any more"
「これ以上悩むな」
"come with me to this city"
「私と一緒にこの街に来てください」

But the young Fisherman did not answer his Soul
しかし、若い漁師は彼の魂に答えませんでした
he closed his lips with the seal of silence
彼は沈黙の封印で唇を閉じた
and he bound his own hands with a tight cord
そして、自分の手をきつく縛った
and he journeyed back to from where he had come
そして、もと来たところへ帰っていきました
he journeyd back to the little bay
彼は小さな湾に戻った
and he journeyed to where his love had sung for him
そして、彼は自分の愛が彼のために歌った場所へと旅をしました
His Soul tried to tempt him along the way
彼の魂は途中で彼を誘惑しようとしました
but he made his Soul no answer
しかし、彼は自分の魂に答えを作らなかった
and he did none of his Soul's wickedness
そして、彼は自分の魂の邪悪さを一切行わなかった
so great was the power of the love that was within him
彼の中にあった愛の力は、とても大きかったのです
when he reached the shore he loosened the cord
岸に着くと、紐を緩めました
and he took the seal of silence from his lips
そして彼は唇から沈黙の封印を剥がした
he called out to the little Mermaid

彼は人魚姫に声をかけました
But she did not answer his call for her
しかし、彼女は彼の呼びかけに答えませんでした
she did not answer, although he called all day
彼は一日中電話をかけたが、彼女は答えなかった
his Soul mocked the young Fisherman
彼の魂は若い漁師を嘲笑した
"you have little joy out of thy love"
「あなたの愛から、あなたは少しの喜びしか得られません」
"you are pouring water into a broken vessel"
「壊れた器に水を注いでいる」
"you have given away what you had"
「あなたは自分が持っていたものを手放した」
"but nothing has been given to you in return"
「しかし、見返りには何も与えられていない」
"It would be better if you came with me"
「一緒に来てくれた方がいいのに」
"because I know where the Valley of Pleasure lies"
「快楽の谷がどこにあるか知っているから」
But the young Fisherman did not answer his Soul
しかし、若い漁師は彼の魂に答えませんでした

in a cleft of the rock he built himself a house
岩の裂け目に、彼は自分で家を建てました
and he abode there for the space of a year
そして、彼は一年間そこに住んだ
every morning he called to the Mermaid
毎朝、彼は人魚に呼びかけた
and every noon he called to her again
そして、正午ごとに、彼は再び彼女を呼んだ
and at night-time he spoke her name
そして夜になると、彼は彼女の名前を口にした
but she never rose out of the sea to meet him
しかし、彼女は彼に会うために海から上がることはありませんでした
and he could not find her anywhere in the sea
そして、海のどこにも彼女を見つけることができませんでし

た
he sought for her in the caves
彼は洞窟で彼女を探しました
he sought for her in the green water
彼は緑の水の中で彼女を探しました
he sought for her in the pools of the tide
彼は潮の池で彼女を探しました
and he sought for her in the wells
そして、井戸で娘を探しました
the wells that are at the bottom of the deep
深海の底にある井戸
his Soul didn't stop tempting him with evil
彼の魂は悪で彼を誘惑するのをやめませんでした
and it whispered terrible things to him
そして、それは彼に恐ろしいことをささやきました
but his Soul could not prevail against him
しかし、彼の魂は彼に打ち勝つことができませんでした
the power of his love was too great
彼の愛の力はあまりにも大きかった

after the year was over the Soul thought within itself
一年が過ぎた後、魂はそれ自身の中に考えた
"I have tempted my master with evil"
「わたしは主人を悪で誘惑した」
"but his love is stronger than I am"
「しかし、彼の愛は私よりも強い」
"I will tempt him now with good"
「今、善をもって彼を誘惑しよう」
"it may be that he will come with me"
「もしかしたら、一緒に来てくれるかもしれない」
So he spoke to the young Fisherman
そこで彼は若い漁師に話しかけました
"I have told thee of the joy of the world"
「わたしは世の喜びをあなたに告げた」
"and thou hast turned a deaf ear to me"
「そして、あなたは私に耳を傾けなかった」
"allow me to tell thee of the world's pain"

「世界の苦しみを汝に伝えさせてください」
"and it may be that you will listen"
「そして、あなたが耳を傾けてくれるかもしれません」
"because pain is the Lord of this world"
「痛みはこの世の主だから」
"and there is no one who escapes from its net"
「そして、その網から逃れる者はいない」
"There be some who lack raiment"
「着物に乏しい者もいる」
"and there are others who lack bread"
「また、パンに事欠く者もいる」
"There are widows who sit in purple"
「紫色に坐るやもめがいる」
"and there are widows who sit in rags"
「ぼろをまとって座っているやもめがいる」
"The beggars go up and down on the roads"
「物乞いは道を上り下りする」
"and the pockets of the beggars are empty"
「そして、乞食のポケットは空っぽです」
"Through the streets of the cities walks famine"
「都市の通りを通って飢饉が歩く」
"and the plague sits at their gates"
「そして疫病は彼らの門に座っている」
"Come, let us go forth and mend these things"
「さあ、出て行って、これらのものを繕おう」
"let us make these things be different"
「これらを違うものにしましょう」
"why should you wait here calling to thy love?"
「なぜここで待っていなければならないのですか、あなたの愛を呼び求めてください。」
"she will not come to your call"
「彼女はあなたの電話に来ません」
"And what is love?"
「では、愛とは何でしょうか?」
"And why do you value it so highly?"
「それで、どうしてそんなに高く評価するんですか?」
But the young Fisherman didn't answer his Soul

しかし、若い漁師は彼の魂に答えませんでした
so great was the power of his love
彼の愛の力は大きかった
And every morning he called to the Mermaid
そして毎朝、人魚に呼びかけました
and every noon he called to her again
そして、正午ごとに、彼は再び彼女を呼んだ
and at night-time he spoke her name
そして夜になると、彼は彼女の名前を口にした
Yet never did she rise out of the sea to meet him
しかし、彼女が彼に会うために海から上がることはありませんでした
nor in any place of the sea could he find her
また、海のどの場所でも、彼は彼女を見つけることができませんでした
though he sought for her in the rivers of the sea
彼は海の川で彼女を探したが
and in the valleys that are under the waves
そして波の下にある谷で
in the sea that the night makes purple
夜が紫色に染まる海で
and in the sea that the dawn leaves grey
歌詞の意味: 夜明けが灰色を残す海で

after the second year was over
2年目が終わってから
the Soul spoke to the young Fisherman at night-time
魂は夜、若い漁師に話しかけました
while he sat in the wattled house alone
彼は一人でワトルドハウスに座っていました
"I have tempted thee with evil"
「わたしは悪をもってあなたを誘惑した」
"and I have tempted thee with good"
「わたしは善をもってあなたを誘惑した」
"and thy love is stronger than I am"
「あなたの愛は私よりも強い」
"I will tempt thee no longer"

「もうあなたを誘惑しない」
"but please, allow me to enter thy heart"
「しかし、どうか、私があなたの心に入ることを許してください」
"so that I may be one with thee, as before"
「わたしが前と同じようにあなたと一つになるため」
"thou mayest enter," said the young Fisherman
「入っていいぞ」と若い漁師は言いました
"because when you had no heart you must have suffered"
「心がなかったら苦しんだに違いないから」
"Alas!" cried his Soul
「ああ!」彼の魂は叫んだ
"I can find no place of entrance"
「入り口が見つからない」
"so compassed about with love is this heart of thine"
「愛を込めて、この心は汝の心である」
"I wish that I could help thee," said the young Fisherman
「おまえの役に立てたらいいのに」と若い漁師は言いました
while he spoke there came a great cry of mourning from the sea
彼が話している間に、海から大きな嘆きの叫び声が聞こえてきました
the cry that men hear when one of the Sea-folk is dead
海の民の一人が死んだときに人が聞く叫び声
the young Fisherman leapt up and left his house
若い漁師は跳び上がって家を出ました
and he ran down to the shore
そして岸に駆け下りた
the black waves came hurrying to the shore
黒い波が岸に急いでやってきた
the waves carried a burden that was whiter than silver
波は銀よりも白い重荷を運んでいた
it was as white as the surf
波のように白かった
and it tossed on the waves like a flower
そしてそれは花のように波に翻弄された
And the surf took it from the waves

そして、波は波からそれを奪った
and the foam took it from the surf
そして、泡は波からそれを奪いました
and the shore received it
そして岸はそれを受け取った
lying at his feet was the body of the little Mermaid
彼の足元には人魚姫の死体が横たわっていた
She was lying dead at his feet
彼女は彼の足元に死んで横たわっていた
he flung himself beside her, and wept
彼は彼女のそばに身を投げ出し、泣きました
he kissed the cold red of her mouth
彼は彼女の口の冷たい赤にキスをした
and he stroked the wet amber of her hair
そして濡れた琥珀色の髪を撫でた
he wept like someone trembling with joy
彼は喜びに震える人のように泣いた
in his brown arms he held her to his breast
彼は茶色の腕の中で彼女を胸に抱きしめた
Cold were the lips, yet he kissed them
唇は冷たかったが、彼はそれにキスをした
salty was the honey of her hair
塩辛いのは彼女の髪の蜂蜜だった
yet he tasted it with a bitter joy
それでも、彼は苦い喜びでそれを味わった
He kissed her closed eyelids
彼は彼女の閉じた瞼にキスをした
the wild spray that lay upon her was less salty than his tears
彼女に降り注ぐ荒々しい水しぶきは、彼の涙よりも塩辛くなかった
to the dead little mermaid he made a confession
死んだ人魚姫に、彼は告白をした
Into the shells of her ears he poured the harsh wine of his tale
彼女の耳殻に、彼は自分の物語の厳しいワインを注いだ
He put the little hands round his neck
彼は小さな手を首に回した

and with his fingers he touched the thin reed of her throat
そして指で彼女の喉の細い葦に触れた
his joy was bitter and deep
彼の喜びは苦く、深いものだった
and his pain was full of a strange gladness
そして、その痛みは奇妙な喜びに満ちていた
The black sea came nearer
黒海が近づいてきた
and the white foam moaned like a leper
白い泡はハンセン病患者のようにうめき声をあげた
the sea grabbed at the shore with its white claws of foam
海は白い泡の爪で岸を掴んだ
From the palace of the Sea-King came the cry of mourning again
海王の宮殿から、再び嘆きの叫びが聞こえてきた
far out upon the sea the great Tritons could be heard
遥か海の向こうで、大きなトリトンの声が聞こえた
they blew hoarsely upon their horns
彼らはかすれた声で角を吹いた
"Flee away," said his Soul
「逃げろ」と魂が言った
"if the sea comes nearer it will slay thee"
「海が近づいたら、お前を殺す」
"please, let us leave, for I am afraid"
「どうか、お帰りにしましょう。怖いので」
"because thy heart is closed against me"
「あなたの心はわたしに対して閉ざされているからである」
"out of the greatness of thy love I beg you
「あなたの愛の偉大さゆえに、私はあなたに懇願します
"flee away to a place of safety"
「安全な場所に逃げる」
"Surely you would not do this to me again?"
「まさか、もう二度と私にこんなことはしないの?」
"do not send me into another world without a heart"
「心のない別の世界に私を送り込まないでください」
the young Fisherman did not listen to his Soul
若い漁師は彼の魂に耳を傾けませんでした

but he spole to the little Mermaid
しかし、彼は人魚姫にスポール
and he said, "Love is better than wisdom"
そして彼は言った、「愛は知恵にまさる」
"love is more precious than riches"
「愛は富よりも尊い」
"love fairer than the feet of the daughters of men"
「人の娘の足よりも美しい愛」
"The fires of the world cannot destroy love"
「世界の火は愛を滅ぼすことはできない」
"the waters of the sea cannot quench love"
「海の水は愛を消すことができない」
"I called on thee at dawn"
「夜明けに汝を呼んだ」
"and thou didst not come to my call"
「そして、あなたは私の呼びかけに来なかった」
"The moon heard thy name"
「月は汝の名を聞いた」
"but the moon didn't answer me"
「しかし、月は私に答えなかった」
"I left thee in order to do evil"
「わたしは悪を行なうために、あなたを捨てた」
"and I have suffered for what I've done"
「そして、私は自分のしたことのために苦しんできた」
"but my love for you has never left me"
「でも、あなたへの愛は私から離れなかった」
"and my love was always strong"
「そして私の愛はいつも強かった」
"nothing prevailed against my love"
「私の愛に勝るものは何もなかった」
"though I have looked upon evil"
「わたしは悪を見たが」
"and I have looked upon good"
「わたしは善を見た」
"now that thou are dead, I will also die with thee"
「お前が死んだ今、私もお前と共に死ぬ」
his Soul begged him to depart

彼の魂は彼に去るよう懇願した
but he would not leave, so great was his love
しかし、彼は去ろうとはしませんでした、彼の愛は大きかったです
the sea came nearer to the shore
海が岸に近づいてきた
and the sea sought to cover him with its waves
海は波で彼を覆おうとした
the young Fisherman knew that the end was at hand
若い漁師は、終わりが近づいていることを知っていました
he kissed the cold lips of the Mermaid
彼は人魚の冷たい唇にキスをした
and the heart that was within him broke
そして、彼の中にあった心が壊れた
from the fullness of his love his heart did break
彼の愛の豊かさから、彼の心は壊れました
the Soul found an entrance, and entered his heart
魂は入り口を見つけ、彼の心に入りました
his Soul was one with him, just like before
彼の魂は、以前と同じように、彼と一つでした
And the sea covered the young Fisherman with its waves
そして、海は若い漁師をその波で覆いました

Blessings
祝福

in the morning the Priest went forth to bless the sea
朝、祭司は海を祝福するために出かけました
because the Priest had been troubled that night
その夜、司祭が悩んでいたからです
the monks and the musicians went with him
僧侶や音楽家も一緒に行きました
and the candle-bearers came with the Priest too
そして、ろうそくを運ぶ人たちも司祭と一緒に来ました
and the swingers of censers came with the Priest
香炉を振り回す者たちが司祭と一緒にやってきた
and a great company of people followed him
そして、大勢の人々が彼に従った
when the Priest reached the shore he saw the young Fisherman
僧侶が岸に着くと、若い漁師が見えました
he was lying drowned in the surf
彼は波に溺れて横たわっていた
clasped in his arms was the body of the little Mermaid
その腕には人魚姫の死体が握りしめられていた
And the Priest drew back frowning
そして司祭は眉をひそめて後ずさった
he made the sign of the cross and exclaimed aloud:
彼は十字架のしるしをし、大声で叫びました。
"I will not bless the sea, nor anything that is in it"
「わたしは海も、海にあるものも祝福しない」
"Accursed be the Sea-folk and those who traffic with them"
「海の民と彼らと交易する者たちは呪われよ」
"And as for the young Fisherman;"
「それで、若い漁師は」
"he forsook God for the sake of love"
「彼は愛のために神を捨てた」
"and now he lays here with his lover"
「そして今、彼は恋人と一緒にここに横たわっている」
"he was slain by God's judgement"

「彼は神の裁きによって殺された」
"take up his body and the body of his lover"
「彼の体と彼の恋人の体を取り上げなさい」
"bury them in the corner of the Field"
「野原の隅に埋めろ」
"let no mark of why they were be set above them"
「なぜ彼らが彼らの上に置かれたのか、そのしるしをすべきではない」
"don't give them any sign of any kind"
「彼らにいかなる種類の兆候も与えないでください」
"none shall know the place of their resting"
「だれも彼らの安息の所を知ることはできない」
"because they were accursed in their lives"
「人生で呪われたから」
"and they shall be accursed in their deaths"
「そして、彼らはその死において呪われるであろう」
And the people did as he commanded them
民は命じられたとおりにした
in the corner of the field where no sweet herbs grew
甘いハーブが生えていない畑の片隅に
they dug a deep pit for their graves
彼らは墓のために深い穴を掘りました
and they laid the dead things within the pit
そして、死んだものを穴の中に置いた

when the third year was over
3年目が終わったとき
on a day that was a holy day
聖なる日だった日に
the Priest went up to the chapel
僧侶は礼拝堂に上がった
he went to show the people the wounds of the Lord
彼は民に主の傷を見せに行った
and he spoke to them about the wrath of God
そして、神の怒りについて彼らに話した
he bowed himself before the altar
彼は祭壇の前でひれ伏した

he saw the altar was covered with strange flowers
祭壇が奇妙な花で覆われているのが見えた
flowers that he had never seen before
今まで見たことのない花
they were strange to look at
見るからに奇妙だった
but they had an interesting kind beauty
しかし、彼らは興味深い親切な美しさを持っていました
their beauty troubled him in a strange way
その美しさは奇妙な方法で彼を悩ませた
their odour was sweet in his nostrils
その匂いは彼の鼻孔に甘かった
he felt glad, but he did not understand why
彼はうれしく感じたが、その理由はわからなかった
he began to speak to the people
彼は人々に語り始めた
he wanted to speak to them about the wrath of God
彼は神の怒りについて彼らに話したかったのです
but the beauty of the white flowers troubled him
しかし、白い花の美しさは彼を悩ませました
and their odour was sweet in his nostrils
そして、その匂いは彼の鼻孔に甘かった
and another word came onto his lip
そして、別の言葉が彼の唇に浮かびました
he did not speak about the wrath of God
彼は神の怒りについて語らなかった
but he spoke of the God whose name is Love
しかし、彼は愛という名の神について語りました
he did not know why he spoke of this
なぜこんなことを話したのか、彼はわからなかった
when he had finished the people wept
彼が話し終えると、人々は泣いた
the Priest went back to the sacristy
司祭は聖具室に戻った
and his eyes too were full of tears
そして彼の目も涙でいっぱいでした
the deacons came in and began to unrobe him

執事たちが入ってきて、イエスの服を脱ぎ始めました
And he stood as if he was in a dream
そして、まるで夢の中にいるかのように立っていた
"What are the flowers that stand on the altar?"
「祭壇に飾られている花は何ですか?」
"where did they come from?"
「どこから来たの?」
And they answered him
彼らはイエスに答えた
"What flowers they are we cannot tell"
「何の花かはわからない」
"but they come from the corner of the field"
「しかし、彼らは畑の隅からやってくる」
the Priest trembled at what he heard
僧侶はその言葉を聞いて震え上がった
and he returned to his house and prayed
そして家に帰って祈った

in the morning, while it was still dawn
朝、まだ夜明けの頃
the priest went forth with the monks
僧侶は僧侶たちといっしょに出て行きました
he went forth with the musicians
彼は音楽家たちと出かけた
the candle-bearers and the swingers of censers
蝋燭を運ぶ人と香炉を振る人
and he had a great company of people
そして、彼は素晴らしい仲間を持っていました
and he came to the shore of the sea
そして彼は海の岸に着いた
he showed them how he blessed the sea
彼は彼らに、彼が海を祝福する方法を示しました
and he blessed all the wild things that are in it
そして、その中にあるすべての野生のものを祝福しました
he also blessed the fauns
彼はまた、牧神を祝福しました
and he blessed the little things that dance in the woodland

そして、森で踊る小さなものを祝福しました
and he blessed the bright-eyed things that peer through the leaves
そして、木の葉の間から覗く明るい目を祝福しました
he blessed all the things in God's world
彼は神の世界のすべてのものを祝福しました
and the people were filled with joy and wonder
人々は喜びと驚きに満たされた
but flowers never grew again in the corner of the field
しかし、畑の隅に花が咲くことはありませんでした
and the Sea-folk never came into the bay again
そして、海の民は二度と湾に入らなかった
because they had gone to another part of the sea
彼らは海の別の場所に行ってしまったからです

The End
最後です

www.tranzlaty.com

www.ingramcontent.com/pod-product-compliance
Lightning Source LLC
Chambersburg PA
CBHW011952090526
44591CB00020B/2744